T0304971

The Secret Diary
of Queen Camilla

The Secret Diary
of Queen Camilla

Hilary Rose

CONSTABLE

CONSTABLE

First published in Great Britain in 2024 by Constable

1 3 5 7 9 10 8 6 4 2

A CIP catalogue record for this book
is available from the British Library.

ISBN: 978-1-40872-120-9

Typeset in Sabon LT by Hewer Text UK Ltd, Edinburgh
Printed and bound in Great Britain by Clays Ltd, Elcograf S.p.A.

Papers used by Constable are from well-managed
forests and other responsible sources.

Constable
An imprint of
Little, Brown Book Group
Carmelite House
50 Victoria Embankment
London EC4Y 0DZ

An Hachette UK Company
www.hachette.co.uk

www.littlebrown.co.uk

For my parents, who always say I can do it

20th May

Clarence House - the day after the Coronation

'I won't lie,' I say, 'the Koh-i-Noor situation was a disappointment. If a gel's got to flatten her hair with a thumping great crown, then it might as well have a thumping great diamond in the middle. I hoped until I was actually in the carriage that it might get a reprieve.'

'Reprieve from what?' says my darling sister Annabel. 'Being nicked?' and I say actually, Annabel, it wasn't stolen and history is rarely that simple, but she rolls her eyes. She's come over for a Coronation debrief and given me a big leather Smythson diary. It's dark green and has 'Game Set and Match' stamped on the front in gold, above two tennis racquets. I look at her doubtfully.

'I don't play tennis and I haven't written a diary since I was a teenager,' I tell her.

'I know,' she says pleasantly, 'but "game, set and match" seems rather appropriate, don't you think? They

1

had another with "Dreams and Thoughts" on it, but that sounds a bit racy. And writing down your royal life might help keep you normal for real life, so when you talk to me, you can focus on the important things.'

'Such as?' I say.

'Horses,' she replies. 'Dogs. Soft furnishings. How much Chablis there is left in the bottle,' and she upends it into her glass. 'Cheers!'

21st May
Midday

'Why is it always so bally freezing in here?' Annabel asks as the wind whips round the Chinese Chippendale.

'Charles,' I say. 'He goes round opening the windows and turning the thermostat down. If I complain, he stands up, hooks his thumb in his suit pocket and gives it the full King about climate change.' Annabel peers round the room, checks over her shoulder, roots behind the cushions and waggles her toes speculatively under the pouffe.

'He isn't here,' she says. So we close all the windows, except the one where the urn footman has taken up position outside, ready for when I have a precautionary ciggie.

'Precautionary?' asks Annabel, raising an eyebrow.

'I'm making sure the nicotine levels are optimal,' I tell her, 'before I give up,' and she rolls her eyes again and switches on *Bargain Hunt*.

4 o'clock

We're reminiscing about my Coronation dress, which had Bluebell and Beth embroidered on the hem. Darling Bruce, the designer, got very confused and thought they were cats. 'Cats!' I say to Annabel. 'Of course they're not bally cats! What would the dogs think if I had cats embroidered on my Coronation dress?' and we look at Bluebell and Beth and she says well quite, and I exhale smoke over the herbaceous border below the window. Bluebell is shredding the *Racing Post* and Beth is eyeing the footman's ankle speculatively. 'OFF!' I tell her and she backs away and humps the Chippendale instead.

'The trouble with your dogs,' says Annabel thoughtfully, 'is that they savage things first and ask questions later,' and I start to protest then realise she's right. Instead we turn to the Coronation bling and how thrilled the Crown Jeweller was when I told him I'd wear everything he could find and he must check behind the sofas at The Tower just in case. I only ever find shredded copies of the *Racing Post*, I told him, but who knows what might turn up.

'I said to him, "I'll wear it all, bling me up, Scotty!" and he said "But I'm called John",' and Annabel hoots with laughter as I drop my ciggie into the urn outside, and give the footman the thumbs up.

22nd May

Clarence House – 7 a.m.

I'm giving my hair a final flourish of the Elnett at my dressing table when Annabel calls to check on my plans for the day. 'I am at my *toilette*,' I tell her in my grandest voice, and she snorts and asks if it's catching. Charles is hanging upside down from the picture rail, because he says it's good for his spine, or his head, or possibly both. His new private secretary starts today and he's keen to start the day well, beginning with his spine. Or his head.

'Remind me what the new chap's called?' I ask, and he says Clive.

'Wiltshire man,' I ask, 'or Gloucestershire?' and Charles says does it matter? Does it have to be one or the other?

'Of course it bally matters,' I say, pausing the Elnett in mid-air over the wings soaring up the side of my face. 'What if he's from Somerset? Savages, the lot of them.' Charles, who's stopped pretending he's a bat and is at last upright, and much easier to talk to, says that he thinks Clive might be from Devon or possibly Cornwall and I look thoughtfully at him.

'Don't be ridiculous,' I say.

8.30 a.m.

'Sir Clive Alderton for your morning meeting,' announces the footman. I scrutinise him over the top of my reading glasses.

4

'M4 or M5?' I ask and Sir Clive looks at me gravely. 'M4,' he replies.

'Good man,' I tell him, and leave them to it.

That evening

'How did it go with Clive?' I ask Charles. He stands up and puts his thumb in his pocket and opens his mouth to speak and I look at him in disbelief. 'The King thing?' I say. 'Is that strictly necessary? All I asked is how you got on with your new chap.' Just then, the clock strikes six, and Clive walks in with his coat on and Bluebell trotting behind him, closer to his ankle than I'd like.

'OFF!' I bellow and Clive jumps and Bluebell shoots under the pouffe. 'How about a stiffie before you go,' I say, 'to celebrate the end of your first day?' Clive looks from me to Charles and back again and I motion to the footman to pour us all a G&T and lean back against an embroidered cushion which reads 'When Life gives You Lemons, Add Vodka'.

25th May

Lt Col. Jonathan Thompson walks in, bows and asks if we need to be disciplined. Or at least I ~~hope~~ think he does. He definitely walks in, but the rest is hazy because he's so bally handsome. He's Charles's equerry, which is frankly a waste, and the press are calling him the Hot Equerry. As Annabel said, gazing into the middle distance, it's very hard to concentrate with a good-looking young chap in a jaunty kilt about the place.

'Unless he's playing bagpipes under your bedroom window at dawn,' I tell her, 'when all a gel wants is a Marlboro Light not bally "Flower of Scotland".' And besides, I tell her, scanning the instructions on a box of nicotine patches, 'Clarence House is nowhere near Scotland.'

'What would you prefer?' says Annabel. '"Flower of Zone One"?'

27th May

'"Post-Coronation meeting to discuss family personnel categories going forward under the new sovereign",' I read aloud from my schedule. 'Couldn't we summarise it as "friend or foe"?' I ask Clive, but he says the Human Resources department wrote it and they thought 'working' and 'non-working' royals was an outmoded and unfair way of describing people.

'It implies that non-working royals don't work,' he explained.

'But they don't,' I say, and he says quite so.

'Although,' I add, 'Beatrice and Eugenie work very hard at something, or at least Fergie says they do, so it must be true,' and he says quite so, ma'am.

'Will you please stop saying that?' I ask and he stares at the cornice which I've started to notice he does when he's trying not to laugh, but Charles says that can't possibly be right because Clive never laughs. 'He isn't employed to laugh,' he said. 'Quite the opposite.' Anyway, Clive says that HR keep talking about making the CEO more accountable, but the last time that happened in 1649 it ended with the CEO having his head chopped off. He thinks the more distractions they're offered the better for everyone, but especially those of us with ambitions for our bodies to remain attached to our heads.

'You're bally wordy today,' I say and he says it must be the Weetabix, he had three, and I wonder again if he's making a joke.

'These categories,' I say to Charles on the way back from an engagement, 'good idea. Never thought of dealing with family like that.'

'Family? Fight like rats in a sack, the lot of them,' he mutters, shaking his head and I tell him he really shouldn't talk about much-loved family members like that.

'I don't talk about much-loved family members at all,' he says. 'That was my darling Mama. And it caused no end of trouble in California when we forgot.'

28th May

'So what sort of categories are we thinking?' I ask Charles in the morning. 'Useful/Useless? Blonde/Brunette? Royal Lodge/Travelodge?'

He says he doesn't think I'm taking this entirely seriously and I say perish the thought and Clive arrives wearing a hard hat with a folder marked 'The Wider Family: The Way Forward'.

'Very slick,' I say. 'Which am I? Family or foe? And talk me through the hat?'

Clive says it's a precaution, in case the wider family turns up.

'So in future we think in terms of Senior Royals, Everyone Else and Others,' he explains and Charles nods approvingly.

'Which am I?' I ask and Clive says somewhere between working and non-working depending on whether it's racing season. Senior royals are Charles, William and Kate, Everyone Else is Anne, Edward and Sophie and Others are basically the Yorks ('Always been problematic, the Yorks,' said the regius professor of history at Oxford when he came for dinner. 'Even in the fifteenth century they were giving us hell.')

'Anyone else?' I ask brightly.

'Harry and Meghan,' he adds, dropping his voice to a whisper as we always do when it comes to the Sussexes. Walls have ears, he once said, 'or more likely hidden cameras and microphones marked NETFLIX,' I muttered to Charles.

'How does Andrew feel about his family being an Other?' I ask, and Clive says we haven't told him yet. 'Maybe run it up the flagpole at Royal Lodge and find out,' I chuckle and Charles says that isn't funny and will I please start taking this seriously and I head to the window for a gasper then remember I've got four nicotine patches on my arm.

'It's book club for me tonight,' I tell Charles later, 'and we're choosing a new one. I think I might suggest an old classic: *My Family and Other Animals*.'

29th May
Chelsea Flower Show

Coronations are all very well, says Charles, but you can't beat a cloud-pruned hornbeam.

'Or a flowering fruit tree,' he adds, looking wistful, 'and that reminds me, the shrubbery at Highgrove really should be weeded by—' and here he looks around him vaguely.

'A gardener?' I suggest, and he says yes, that's just what he was thinking, a gardener, or someone else who isn't King would be marvellous, if we can find such a person, and I say I'll ask Clive to see to it. I don't give a fig about cloud-pruned hornbeams or any of the other things he talks to Alan Titchmarsh about, but the Chelsea Flower Show's a fixture for The Firm. If you have to look delighted for a living, then you might as well do it for a flowering fruit tree as a new bypass. Alan once asked me what was in my garden at Ray Mill and I said 'Flowers'. He said yes, but what varieties? and I said 'Trees'.

'Give me a horse-box over a box hedge any day,' I told him, 'you know where you are with a horse.' But one must do one's duty so I put on my game face and off we go to Chelsea. 'Should we knight Alan Titchmarsh?' I wonder aloud in the car on the way there. 'Good idea,' says Charles. 'What for?'

'Being lovely?' I say. 'And services to herbaceous borders, especially yours. Oh look, darling, a horse!'

30th May

'Has anyone seen Anne recently?' says Charles and we both look expectantly at Clive, who says he thinks it's been a while and flicks through to the last known reference to her in the Court Circular.

'Ah yes,' he says. 'Goodness me, it was 30th March 2022 to be exact. "The Princess Royal today attended a conference on farming in Oxford followed by a reception for retired sailors of indeterminate but undoubted distinction at St James's Palace. At the request of the Foreign Office, she then proceeded directly on state visits to France, Germany, Spain, Portugal, Albania, Bulgaria, Romania, Sri Lanka, India, China, Japan, Malaysia, a diversity of –stans including Kyrgyzstan and finishing in South Korea. For reasons of cost-efficiency, she will return in the back of a military cargo plane, arriving at RAF Brize Norton at 0900 hours on June 18th 2024. Her Royal Highness will then proceed to the opening of a new scout hut in Cirencester."'

'Was it really 2022?' says Charles. 'How time flies . . .'

'Unless you're in the back of a cargo plane,' I say. 'It probably drags a bit then,' and Charles says god bless Anne, whatever would we do without her?

'More,' I mutter.

'South Korea, you say?' Charles asks Clive, and Clive nods. 'Remarkable. Quite remarkable. Let's have her over for dinner when she's finished at the scout hut.'

'Out of interest, are we off anywhere else this year to fly the flag?' I ask Clive, who says that yes, we're due to be spending forty-eight hours in Italy next year.

'Splendid,' says Charles.

I raise an eyebrow. 'So Anne spends two years in the back of a cargo plane and we go to Amalfi for dinner?'

'Not quite, ma'am,' says Clive, 'there will be diplomatic receptions and factory visits and many and varied opportunities to look delighted in circumstances of extreme dullness,' so I put my feet up and reach for the coffee-table book about the Crown Jewels and start sticking Post-it notes marked 'Amalfi' in the chapter on sapphires.

'Lovely lemons in Amalfi,' says Charles to no one in particular.

'Would now also be a good time to discuss Your Majesties' trip to New Zealand, Australia and Samoa in the autumn?' asks Clive, and Bluebell starts to growl softly.

'I'll take that as a no,' he says, bowing and leaving the room.

It's our first garden party as King and Queen.

'Remember when Meghan came to a garden party?' I say and Charles says really? Are you sure? They got married in May and garden parties don't start 'til June and surely they'd gone by then?

'Surprisingly not,' I say, 'it took longer than that. Annabel thinks it's because Netflix told them they had six hours of primetime to fill and they couldn't do that in a week, but she's a shocking cynic. Anyway, believe it or not, Meghan definitely came to one garden party. After ten minutes, she told Harry she was bored and wanted to leave.'

'And?' says Charles. 'What happened next?'

'Guess,' I say and he thinks about it for a moment.

'Harry said I'm afraid we can't,' he tries, 'and told her it's our duty to stay, this is what royal life is like.'

I roll my eyes. 'Not quite.'

2nd June
Clarence House

Andrew's here. Again.

'I'm available for garden parties,' he says, 'and I look rather splendid in a morning suit. I'll come to the next one.'

Charles and I look at each other, and Clive looks at the cornice.

'What a marvellous idea,' says Charles. 'No.'

3rd June

Clive is here to brief us about our upcoming state visit to France. We were supposed to be going months ago, but they were rioting so we postponed. Clive said the optics were bad.

'Rioting youths and petrol bombs are a bit Northern Ireland for us,' he said.

'Whatever's the matter with the French anyway?' I asked. 'Why are they rioting? They have Provence, how hard can it be?'

Clive says possibly not all of them are in Provence, and I give him a hard stare.

'Out of interest,' I ask, 'what do we tell them when we postpone a trip like this? That we'll swing by some other time?' and Clive says yes, something like that, but he expects the Foreign Office might phrase it slightly differently.

4th June

I tell Clive that Charles has been driving me mad practising his French speech in the bathroom mirror. 'He might need some direction,' I explain, and Clive looks puzzled and says why?

'Well,' I say, 'he starts by bellowing "CITOYENS!",' and Clive turns pale. 'Citizens?' he says. 'Are you sure? But . . . he isn't. And they aren't. Or at least they're not HIS citizens. And if it starts like that, how does it end? With "Vive La Revolution"?'

'Not quite,' I say briskly, 'but you might want to cast your eye over the bit where he gets to Robespierre,' and Clive holds a clammy hand over his eyes and hurries out and I can hear him shouting for back-up all the way down the corridor. I lean out of the window and the footman hurries over with the urn. Today he's wearing a tray round his neck like a 1950s' cigarette girl. 'Marlboro Light, ma'am?' he says pleasantly. 'Or is it more of a B&H day?'

5th June

'The damnedest thing happened today,' says Charles, and I look up from the property porn in *Country Life*. There's a lovely Georgian rectory near the coast that would be perfect for Bluebell and Beth.

'Oh?' I say mildly.

'Yes,' he says. 'Clive arrived in my office with the foreign secretary, the regius professor of modern history at Oxford, Cambridge's leading expert on eighteenth-century France and a 1794 engraving of the guillotine in the Place de la Revolution.'

'Oh?' I say mildly. 'And why was that?'

'They thought I might need some help with my speech to the Assemblée Nationale,' says Charles, looking puzzled, 'and a reminder of some key points about the French Revolution.'

'Oh,' I say mildly. 'Such as what?'

'How it ended,' he says.

6th June

I've ordered 572 cans of Elnett for the French trip in a few weeks, and now we're planning my Look for the state banquet. The jewel man's here from The Tower, and my dresser, and I'm looking critically at myself in a full-length mirror. I'm wearing the diamond diadem with a tiara on top, diamond chandelier earrings, matching diamond bracelets stacked up both arms, a diamond necklace the size of the small Indian state it was possibly stolen from and what I like to think is the *pièce de résistance*: a diamond stomacher last worn by Queen Mary. 'Which fool decided stomachers were unfashionable?' I say approvingly to my reflection, and call Annabel. 'I'm festooned in diamonds from head to foot,' I tell her happily, 'not counting the cheeky diamante anklet I bought on Etsy, which Charles simply adores.'

'Too much bling?' I ask the jewel man. 'Or just right?' and the dresser looks at the jewel guy and the jewel guy looks at the floor.

'Just right, then,' I say happily.

7th June

I pop into the staff quarters to check on morale. The footman is pouring Clive's deputy, Chris, a stiff drink.

'Oh dear,' I say, 'has Bluebell misbehaved again with your ankle? I'm awfully sorry.'

But for once, Bluebell's in the clear. Poor Chris was about to start briefing the press about the higher purpose of the French trip when he noticed that some-one had tampered with his notes. The footman passes me the briefing and I start to read.

'The state visit will celebrate Britain's relationship with France,' it begins, which seems fairly uncontro-versial, but then someone's inserted different words. 'Although in point of fact, we don't have one, because we ripped it up with Brexit and it will take genera-tions to repair, and for what? The trip will mark our shared histories,' I read on, 'including bloody revolu-tions which both ended with a dead king – Good vibes! – our shared culture of unreadable seven-teenth-century playwrights, and our many shared values, except collaboration, which is more of a French thing.'

Across the bottom of the paper the culprit has scrawled 'Vive La Revolution! Vive La République!'

'But this is terrible,' I say to Chris. 'I know,' he says. 'Imagine if I'd accidentally read it out to the press. World wars have started over less.'

'Not that,' I say impatiently, 'there's a republican in the building! Call the police!'

8th June

I walk past Charles's office, and Clive's in there on his own looking furtive so I pause. I watch as he discreetly palms a book on Robespierre off Charles's desk and lobs it smoothly underarm to a footman, who puts it in the log basket. I smile and give him the thumbs up, and walk on.

9th June

I'm flicking through the book about the Crown Jewels, marking the pages that catch my eye with bright pink Post-it notes.

'If I've learned one thing in my life,' I say to Charles, 'it's that you can never tell when a state banquet might come along. Preparation,' I say, pointing at the book, 'is key.'

'I don't see the connection,' he says, 'between state banquets and the Crown Jewels. I thought state banquets were when the government orders us to have dinner with ghastly waxworks who've been running small African countries for generations?'

'Or people who had a bally great oil well spout up under their tent,' I say and we chuckle and Clive, who's just walked in, looks horrified and says that really won't look very good in the fly-on-the-wall and we freeze.

'Fly-on-the-wall?' I say, recovering my composure first.

'Relax,' says Clive, 'there isn't one. But someone's probably bugging you, even if it's only Andrew, so it might be a good idea to be a little—'

'Self-censoring?' I interject.

'Silent until spoken to?' says Charles witheringly.

'Circumspect,' says Clive firmly.

'Anyway,' I say, tapping the book, 'these jewels. Have I got the run of them? Or am I getting all excited only to find we nicked them from somewhere and the jewel man's having a hernia?'

Clive looks pained. 'When you describe these exquisite examples of craftsmanship as "nicked",' he says carefully, 'I think that you mean "gifted to us by grateful nations whom we happened to visit, heavily armed, remaining sometimes for many hundreds of years".'

'Yes, yes,' I say airily, 'I expect that's exactly what I mean if you say so, but let's get down to the nitty-gritty: when can I wear the diamond diadem and will you take half the rocks out before I do, like you did with my crown? Also, that tiara Beatrice wore when she got married. I've got my eye on that. Although frankly how on earth that was allowed to happen is beyond me,' and Clive starts to say something about Covid and blood princesses and I give him a quelling look and he stops.

19

'And,' I say, turning to page 274 of the book and holding it up to show him, 'this tiara with the slabs of aquamarine? Yum yum.'

10th June

Planning meeting for the state banquet at Versailles. I'll be wearing a full-length coat dress with a zip up the front and lots of elegant embroidery by darling Bruce, who did my dress for the Coronation and can't tell the difference between dogs and cats.

'There are bad vibes at Versailles for people like us,' I told him. 'Even Anne was spooked, and that was thirty years ago. Although thinking about it, in a straight fight between her and Robespierre, no weapons, I'd put my money on her. What do you think?' and Bruce looks non-committal and I make a mental note to see if Paddy Power offers odds on it. Bruce says could we stick to the task in hand? 'Quite so,' I say. 'Let's keep the look light and pretty and could you possibly embroider darling Blu—' and Bruce looks at me and says, 'No. No dogs or cats or names of grandchildren like at the Coronation. No embroidered flowers of France or Wiltshire or whatever it was you were going to suggest. Plain and elegant,' and I concede defeat gracefully.

For a moment we sit together in amicable silence, me watching *Below Deck Med*, Bruce sketching ideas. 'How about Ray Mill?' I say brightly during the ad break. 'In red, white and blue, round the hem?'

11th June
Paris – state visit, Day 1

So we arrive and do the big exchange of diplomatic gifts.

'What are we giving them?' Charles asked Clive on the way over.

'The Crown Jewels,' I joked, 'they haven't got any of their own,' but nobody laughed.

'Ma'am,' said Clive, who seems to have lost his *joie de vivre*, 'could we not make any jokes about the Crown Jewels while we're here? Or the Revolution?' And I say yes, quite so, and besides, the Crown Jewels are no laughing matter. 'They can keep their grubby hands off until I've got mine on those bally aquamarines,' I say.

'Do I need to repeat myself?' says Charles, ignoring me and looking tetchy and Clive and I both say, 'Why? What did you say?' and he looks even crosser.

'I asked,' he says with exaggerated patience, 'what we're giving the French?'

'You chose exceptionally well, sir,' says Clive, and Charles, who had nothing whatever to do with it, looks mollified. 'We're giving them a large photo of Your Majesties in a solid silver frame and a copy of Voltaire's *Lettres sur les Anglais*.'

'Did they ask for that?' I ask. 'A framed picture of us?' Charles looks at me, astonished.

'Darling,' he says, 'Clive isn't Father Christmas. The French diplomatic service doesn't write a letter saying

21

"Please can you bring us a new book and a photo-graph" and post it up the chimney. Our ambassador and their ambassador decide what will be most appropriate.'

I look at Clive and wonder what he might look like in a Father Christmas hat. 'Is there anything wrong, ma'am?' he says, looking uncomfortable and I say no, not at all, Happy Christmas! then I realise I said that bit out loud.

12th June

We're staying at the British Embassy, which is a pity. I'm more of a George V sort of girl. However, on the plus side, the embassy is on the Rue St Honoré, 'And by happy chance,' I tell Charles, 'that's where Chanel is. I don't suppose I could pop in there before we start work and have a quick mooch?' Charles says no, he doesn't suppose that I can, and I sigh. Anyway, he's gone off to look at some Froggy windfarm. 'Does it run on Camembert?' I joke to Clive and he says no, ma'am, it runs on wind, and I sigh again and think this is going to be a long trip. But now I'm with Brigitte Macron and the work begins. We're about to go out and talk about our exciting new Franco–British literary prize, which I think must be for things which are written with alternate words in French and English.

'Tell me,' I say to Brigitte, 'do you have Elnett in France? Or something even better? One reads all these things in *Grazia* about French pharmacies. And your hair!' and here I give her a conspiratorial wink of mid-life solidarity. 'That isn't just thickening shampoo and back-combing, is it? It's extensions. Am I right or am I right?' and Brigitte turns to the translator for help and he shrugs and out we go.

'I'm a strong advocate for literacy,' I tell the press and guests, 'especially if it's in English. Can't speak a bally word of your lingo. No head for languages at all. Never mind, anything worth reading is in English anyway,' and the room falls silent.

'Molière?' says a French journalist tentatively.

'Who?' I say. 'Does he make thickening shampoo?'

13th June

I call Brigitte after breakfast. 'Bridge,' I say, 'I can call you Bridge, can't I?' and she makes a sort of strangulated sound which I assume is 'Yes' in French. 'I'm just calling to check that our clothes won't clash,' I say. 'I'm going to be in a bright red coat dress with a zip up the front, *comme d'habi*-normal as you say in France, with a white blouse and a blue hat. Red, white and blue! See what I'm doing there? How about you? What colour are you wearing?' and Brigitte makes a sort of snorting noise and I say 'Bless you.'

'You come dressed as British Airways,' she says. 'Interesting. Our flag also is bleu, blanc, rouge, 'owever I will be in white Louis Vuitton 'ead to toe. *Très chic.* My bag is Chanel. My jewellery is *haute*.'

'Splendid,' I say, 'see you at the town hall for the ribbon cutting!' and she makes a non-committal noise which I take to be excitement in French. Filthy language. How they ever learn to speak it is beyond me.

'*Bonjour!*' says Charles brightly, wandering in. '*Comment allez-vous?*' and I look sharply at him and tell him to wash his mouth out with soapy water.

That evening, at the Palace of Versailles

It's the state banquet and Mick Jagger's here.

'Why was he invited?' I ask Bridge and she shrugs.

'Because you're 'oping for a singalong after dinner?' she suggests, and I tell her that's a bally good idea. When I meet Mick later I ask him if he can start with 'Honky Tonk Women' and he looks confused and says he hasn't brought his microphone. 'Or "You Can't Always Get What You Want"?' I say, pointing at the ruby tiara on my head where the aquamarines should be, except the Crown Jeweller said they might have been nicked from the French so better not. Mick looks at Clive.

'I know,' I tell him, '"Livin' on a Prayer", it's my favourite,' and Clive looks mortified, apologises and hustles me away. 'Did I say something wrong?' I ask. 'What about "Rio"? Do you think he knows that one?'

14th June

Versailles is surprisingly impressive if you like that sort of thing. It's all a bit gold and Froggy for me and god knows how much Windolene they get through in the Hall of Mirrors. 'I hope they don't buy supermarket-own brands,' I said to Annabel on the phone. 'It streaks like mad. Also,' I add, 'the banquet. One word. Garlic,' and Annabel says oh dear, and did anyone have a string of onions round their neck and a beret? and I say, no, I don't think so, and she says then how do you know for sure you were in France? You could have been in Germany. Or Devon.

'The garlic would never have happened on your mother's watch,' I tell Charles reproachfully. 'It was always in her rider: no garlic.' Charles looks cross.

'Her Late Majesty my darling Mama did not have riders,' he says. 'She was not some Bon Jovi tribute act. She had certain wishes which were discreetly respected.'

'Of course,' I say, waving a hand airily, 'but either way, call Clive and tell him to put extra toothpaste on your brush, and did we bring the industrial-strength Listerine? The one that takes the roof off your mouth?'

15th June

Last day of the state visit

Staying at the embassy is all very well, I say to Charles, but where's the bally urn footman when you need him? and Charles mutters something non-committal and goes looking for a picture rail to hang off. I tried a sneaky one out the window, but all the fire alarms went off.

'Could you train someone up?' I asked the ambassador. 'With the urns?' He looked confused and over at Clive for guidance, who pretended not to notice. I said oh don't worry about it, I expect I can have one later in the loo on the Eurostar, and we headed out to the car. Emmy and Bridge turn up to wave us off at the Gare du Nord. 'Bally dump,' I mutter to Charles without moving my lips as we get out of the car in front of the station. '*Chère* Brigitte,' says Charles smoothly, leaning in for a double kiss. Bridge told me earlier on the phone that she'd be wearing an ice-blue Dior couture skirt suit, Chanel slingbacks 'and my jewellery will be—' she started to say, and I said 'Wait! Don't tell me! *Haute?*' and she said *Mais oui!*

'I'm practically bilingual,' I told Clive. 'How's that for an *entente cordiale?*' The Dior skirt suit's alright in the flesh, a bit straight up and down for my liking, but then so's her hair. 'I'm more of a fit-and-flare girl,' I told her, gesturing to my wings under their protective wall of Elnett, and my new flared coat dress with a zip up the front. Bridge smiles politely and asks if we've enjoyed ourselves. 'It's been marvellous,' I say. 'Viva France! Viva the repub—' and Clive pokes me sharply in the ribs. 'Lovely trip,' I tell her, 'but I can't wait to get home. You know how it is when you go abroad, the toast's always a bit odd, croissants are overrated, brioche is filthy stuff and you can't get a decent cup of tea,' and the man from the Foreign Office sways and I ask if he's OK.

'I'd like the party to move quite quickly towards the platform,' he says with the gentlest and most diplomatic of shoves. 'We wouldn't want to miss the train, now, would we?'

18th June
Clarence House

We're back in London having a post-trip briefing with the team. Clive and Chris are here and a tiny little man who looks vaguely familiar.

'Who are you?' I ask him. 'The prime minister,' he says. 'Rishi Sunak.'

'Ah, excellent,' I say, 'I've been wanting to meet you but Charles hogs you to himself every week. Does he bore on about Poundbury? Anyway,' I say, giving him a firm tap on the shoulder, 'you need to be doing much more about animal rescue,' and he blinks and takes a step back. 'It's quite shocking how many animals need loving new forever homes, but you have all these bally people,' and I wave wildly in the direction of Notting

Hill, 'paying thousands of pounds for "designer dogs" which match their bally sofas and it's absolutely bally DISGRACEFUL,' and I pause to take a breath and realise the room has fallen silent and everyone's looking strangely at me.

'Urn, ma'am?' says the footman. 'Yes,' I say, shooting the prime minister a dirty look. 'I think it might be a B&H day.'

21st June

We're having the first meeting to discuss Charles's Christmas speech. 'I am not,' says Charles firmly, 'describing people we can't abide as "much-loved members of the family".'

'You shouldn't talk about Andrew like that, and say you can't abide him,' I say. 'He's ghastly, of course, but he is also your brother.'

'I didn't mean Andrew,' he says, 'or at least not him specifically. And it's not just him. I was thinking of almost everyone apart from you,' and I aim for an abashed expression and fail. Tried it before in front of the mirror, actually, but can't pull it off. Abashed doesn't suit me. Anyway, Clive says it's very important to give the impression of being a loving and united family with the best interests of the nation at heart and Charles mutters something about rats in a sack and I snort and Clive looks disapproving and starts on at us again.

'Oh Clive,' I sigh, 'do cut the diplomatic guff, will you? Just occasionally? In private?' and he looks cross and Charles pats his arm and says 'There there, she doesn't mean it really,' and I say I do, actually, because I'm feeling ratty today, and the footman seizes the moment and opens the window and I smile at him gratefully.

22nd June
Highgrove

To Gatcombe Park for lunch with Anne. I'm taking her a giant bottle of duty-free Gordon's gin from the Gare du Nord.

'It'll be super-casual,' Anne tells me over the phone, 'just you, me and the horses.' When I arrive, she's laying the table in the stables and wearing jodhpurs held up with string.

'Awfully good to see you,' she says, waving a pitch-fork at me as the butler arrives with the G&Ts. 'Were you mounted this morning?' she says cheerfully. 'Or did you come by car? I thought all we're going to do is talk about horses,' she continues, gesturing at the table, 'so we might as well cut out the middleman and have lunch WITH them.' She strokes the nose of a lovely bay with one hand and hoists up her jodhpurs with the other and the string snaps. 'Oh, bugger off,' she says to no one in particular and I put my fingers in my mouth and whis-tle, even though Charles hates it when I do that. A foot-man comes scurrying round the corner with an urn. 'Not the urn,' I tell him, 'not so close to the horses. Bad for their lungs. What we actually need is string for the Princess Royal's trousers. Or,' I turn to Anne, 'just a thought, but how about a new pair of jodhpurs?' She looks puzzled and says, 'Why? Nothing wrong with these,' and feeds a carrot to the horse and I shrug, take a swig of my G&T and say 'String it is, then' to the footman and he scurries off to get it.

'Oh, look,' I say happily as a groom rounds the corner, 'another horse!'

That evening

I arrive back at Highgrove from Gatcombe to find Charles sitting on a wicker peacock chair in a vast Indian-style tented pavilion. The footmen have put up Rajasthani lanterns and scattered silk cushions over the floor. He's wearing a Paisley silk robe and has a clear sightline towards the topiary, which he finds reassuring. Except when he remembers the time William and Harry wee-ed on it when they were little and it turned yellow overnight and took years to recover. I survey my darling husband with fond amusement.

'Tent,' I say. 'Interesting choice. And a punkhawallah too,' glancing at the footman who's wafting a large ostrich feather fan above Charles's head, and perspiring gently.

'Oddly enough, that's exactly what Clive said, "Interesting choice",' says Charles, 'but the footmen were bored with no urns to see to, and one thing led to another, and here I am,' and he pats the peacock throne next to him. 'I'm so glad you're here because I want to talk to you about the Edinburgh Military Tattoo.' I blink.

'The Edinburgh Military Tattoo?' I say carefully.

'Yes,' he says. 'I've been thinking we should make it twice a year, not once, to make the Scots feel more welcome.'

'What?' I say. 'Why? Where? Aren't the Scots already welcome enough in Edinburgh?'

'No, no,' he says, gesturing around at the topiary and the tent and the punkhawallah. 'Here! In England! As much-loved members of the wider family that is the United Kingdom,' and I make a mental note never to leave him on his own again for longer than two hours. Out loud I say, 'What a marvellous idea, darling, you are a true visionary. Nothing will make the Scots feel more welcome and valued members of the Union than two military tattoos a year. Remind me – what exactly *is* a military tattoo?' and Charles looks gratified and says he's missed me. I reach for my ciggies and the punkhawallah drops the fan, gives me the thumbs up and says he's missed me too and trots off for the urn.

26th June

It's been decided that we're going to do a fly-on-the-wall documentary about our year since the Coronation.

'Are we sure that's a good idea?' I ask Clive. 'I thought as a family we were better off seen and not heard.'

'Ah yes,' says Clive, 'but what about if *you're* seen and *other* people are heard?'

'Like who?' I ask. 'The Duke of York? He's been jumping up and down trying to be heard for years, but no good ever came of sitting him in front of a TV camera. Fergie can be relied on to say nice things about us, but then she ruins it by plugging porcelain teapots. And no,' I add, giving Clive a warning look, 'I do NOT want her reading *Budgie the Little Helicopter* on my Reading Room podcast,' and he says I quite understand ma'am, I do tell her, but she can be most insistent. 'Anyway,' I say, 'cut to the chase: who's talking on this programme?' and he says Annabel and Fiona, the Marchioness of Lansdowne, and he presses play on an iPad and up they pop.

'She's bally marvellous,' says Annabel.

'She's bally marvellous,' says Fiona. 'So self-effacing. Such a marvellous sense of humour. So supportive of the King, and not at all interested in cigarettes any more, gave up years ago.' I choke mid-drag.

'Don't worry, this is a rough edit,' says Clive, 'and we have copyright approval. That won't make the final cut.'

'It's not about me,' I say with a straight face, 'or the Silk Cut. I'm just thinking about the urn footman's right to privacy,' and Clive says of course ma'am, no one could doubt it.

27th June

The television people arrived with Part 2 of the documentary. Anne appears on screen saying she's known me 'off and on' for years and I snort. 'Not to mention my ex-husband The Brig in his bachelor days,' I say. 'Did she mention that she'd "known" a certain Brigadier Andrew Parker Bowles on and off for years as well?' and the television people look at Clive for guidance, but he stares at the cornice. Then the Crown Jeweller appears on screen to talk about the crowns.

'I hope he didn't make off with my coffee-table book before he did this, I need it,' I say warningly, and Clive says of course not, the butler wouldn't let it out of the house. I beckon to the footman to open the window and light a ciggie. 'Given up,' I say smugly. 'Easiest thing in the world, as long as you always have a packet to hand. Honestly, people do go on about how hard it is but,' I say, taking a long drag and dropping the butt out of the window, 'I've now given up smoking for, ooh, nearly a minute.' Clive looks at me gravely and says, 'Congratulations ma'am, we're all very proud of you' and ushers the television people out of the room.

'Do you know,' I tell Charles later, 'I think he might have been making a joke,' and Charles says don't be ridiculous.

28th June

Christmas speech planning (2)

'I'm still giving up smoking,' I tell Charles as Clive walks in with sheaves of paper tied with ribbon and a wide selection of fountain pens. 'That's very interesting, ma'am,' he says, 'but perhaps not quite right as a topic for the Christmas speech?' and Charles looks put out and says could we both please concentrate on the matter in hand, which is him?

'When my darling Mama was planning her speech, she always used to consider first what had happened over the year,' he said, 'but all I can remember is my Coronation. Did anything else happen? Anything that might resonate with—' and he waves in the direction of The Mall, and looks expectantly at me and Clive.

'Well, William and Kate made an excellent fist of looking delighted that day in Nottingham,' I say, 'and Sophie really is a trooper, that tree she planted in Milton Keynes is flourishing. As for Anne, well: 4,523 engagements! Travelling invariably by horse and not so much as a new pair of jodhpurs.' Clive asks what relevance the Princess Royal's jodhpurs have to the Christmas speech? I say probably very little, but the seat of them is so threadbare it really should be seen to be believed and he looks appalled at the thought of eyeing the royal seat.

'Or perhaps not,' I say hurriedly.

1st July
Clarence House

After the success of the trip to France, everyone wants to discuss ideas for future state visits. France was all very well because we can get the train, I tell them, but planes are another matter, because what is to stop them from plummeting to earth in a fireball? 'Nothing,' I say to Clive, 'nothing at all.' Clive started to explain the laws of physics, as if physics has anything to do with it. Anyway, now we're in the library and the footman has rolled out a big map of the world on the floor, so we can walk around it and see what's what.

'Or we could play Twister,' I say to Charles, bending over with my feet in Canada and my hands in Belize and looking up at him through my legs. He looks blank and says, 'You'll do your back in, and what's Twister anyway?'

The footman has stuck interesting facts about the major countries on Post-its. 'Too big' it says on China and 'Challenging food,' on somewhere in the Middle

East with unfortunate habits relating to sheep's eyes. 'Unpronounceable' it says on Kyrgyzstan. 'Not terribly enlightening,' I say to Charles, 'but you can't fault the truth of it.' Clive arrives with a whip from the stables to use as a pointer.

'Marvellous choice of accessory,' I tell him, 'everything's better with a whip in your hand.' Clive looks at me and looks at the whip in alarm, and drops it out the window where it falls into the urn. The footman looks at it, then shrugs. Clive explains that the Foreign Office wants us to go somewhere like China or India while we still can, whereas Charles wants to go to Australia. I wander over to Australia on the other side of the room to get a feel for how far it is.

'Too far,' I say, heading up to the Middle East.

'Austria?' says Clive.

'Too damp.'

'India?'

'Too hot.'

'Finland?'

'Too cold.'

'Perhaps we should frame this conversation differently,' says Clive, in slightly strangled tones. 'Where WOULD you be prepared to go, ma'am?' I consider the matter, then give him my most dazzling smile.

'I hear Wiltshire's lovely at this time of year,' I say, stamping on Sweden. 'How about there?'

3rd July
Highgrove

Pointless place. All the box hedging you could want, but no Aga.

'If I'm going to be in Gloucestershire,' I tell Charles, 'then I might as well be in Wiltshire.' He looks perplexed.

'At my own place,' I clarify, and he still looks puzzled.

'Why are you so keen on being at Ray Mill?' he asks, gesturing to the box hedging and the Chinese Chippendale, newly upholstered in a jaunty yellow silk and still about as comfortable as a horse-box. 'Isn't Ray Mill a little . . . lived in?'

'It's a house,' I say. 'People live in it. That's the point.'

Charles considers this. 'Perhaps I meant mucky,' he says. 'Covered in dog hair. And anyway, why do you have to live in your house? I have literally dozens of houses, all over the place, that I hardly ever live in. Never go. Couldn't even tell you where half of them are, and some of them are vast palaces in central London.'

'Yes,' says Clive. 'About those . . .'

5th July

Still at bally Highgrove because Charles wants to finish his first Christmas Day address somewhere he can be sure the pens work. 'And that,' he says, 'means definitely not in London because that's where Penny Mordaunt is.' I explain for the umpteenth time that Penny came with the accession, and she had nothing to do with the malfunctioning pens, but he still looks haunted. 'That sword,' he says. 'So erect, so rigid, for so long. Also, her hair went straight down when hair should go like yours,' and he makes sweeping up and out motions, like wings. We smile fondly at each other and he tries to run his fingers through it but the Elnett repels him and it crackles.

6th July
Ray Mill House, Wiltshire

Charles is decompressing in the topiary at Highgrove, so I've come to Ray Mill for a day or two. The grand-children are running amok, Bluebell is savaging *Horse & Hound*, Beth is humping a cushion embroidered 'Save Water, Drink Champagne' and I'm flicking through a tiara catalogue.

'Anyone in?' says The Brig walking straight in, while my protection officer turns puce. 'I suppose it's too much to hope that you'd knock,' I ask, and he says yes that would indeed be too much to hope, but if I ask nicely he'll find the ashtray and make me a stiff G&T. I tell him that sometimes ex-husbands are quite the most useful thing in the world.

'Unless you're Fergie,' he says.

8th July

It's the inaugural meeting of the Operation Andrew sub-group: me, Charles and Clive. 'We've trying very hard to move him out of Royal Lodge,' says Clive, 'to somewhere that doesn't have royal in the name.'

'Or a flagpole for him to fly the family colours,' mutters the comms woman, and Clive brightens. 'Actually,' he says, 'there's news on that front,' and Charles stops obsessively checking his pen collection for defects and perks up. Clive says there's a promising new commuter estate being built just north of Peterborough. Two beds, two baths and no room for a flagpole. It's close enough that he can't complain he's exiled, far enough that he can't pop in, and well out of drone range, because he's taken to tracking us by drone and popping in 'on the off chance' to ask for money. I once asked the security chap how we know the drone belongs to Andrew and he said 'because it has a flagpole'.

'The problem with Andrew,' says Charles, 'is that he's never commuted anywhere. And whenever he did, it ended badly. Or with someone awful. Or on a golf course.'

'Or on the front page,' says the comms woman, and everyone glares at her and Clive stares impassively out of the window. I decide to take charge and assert myself.

'No,' I tell Charles. 'The problem with Andrew is a) that he lives in a house with a flagpole and b) the last time we sent the bailiffs in—'

'A week last Tuesday,' interjects Clive, consulting his notes, 'at shortly after nine in the morning.'

'Thank you, Clive,' I say, and he bows and I continue. 'A week last Tuesday, at shortly after nine in the morning, he refused to be disturbed because he was eating a breakfast of soft-boiled eggs with crumpet soldiers, wearing the full robes of the Order of the Garter and a plumed hat. And that, my darling husband, is the problem with Andrew,' and Clive carries on staring impassively out of the window, but his mouth twitches.

9th July
Operation Andrew Day 2

We all look at our agendas. 'Article 1. Evicting Andrew from Royal Lodge,' it reads, 'a suggested timeline.'

'Well this should be a bally short meeting,' I say cheerfully, perched on the window seat with my feet up and flicking through a copy of *Hello!*. 'How about we all agree on "today" as the timeline and go straight to the pub?' Clive thanks me for my contribution and I chuckle and look back at the agenda.

Article 2. How to stop Andrew wearing garter robes at every opportunity.
Article 3. How to stop Andrew saying anything out loud ever again.

Article 4. How to prevent Andrew from living
anywhere with a flagpole ever again, and raising
his flag to signal that he's at home.
Article 5. How to stop Andrew full stop.

It's going to be a long morning. I sigh and put my
fingers in my mouth and whistle out of the window,
and the footman comes trotting round the corner with
the urn.

10th July

Operation Andrew is getting to work in the war room.
A huge to-scale map of Windsor Great Park has been
tacked onto a table, with a big red dot on Royal Lodge
and a green one on Frogmore Cottage, where we hope
he might move, and a Plan of Last Resort, involving
the commuter estate just north of Peterborough. There
are big arrows pointing all over the place, like the
opening credits of *Dad's Army*, and a footman is pushing model removal vans around with a paddle in real
time. Clive is wearing a headset and talking urgently
into the mouthpiece. 'Yes, but have you secured the
flag?' he's saying. 'And the pole?' and the person at the
other end obviously says no, they seem to have gone
missing, because Clive looks furious, which is odd
because Clive doesn't usually do fury. 'Well bloody
find them!' he hisses. 'Because if I get to Frogmore and
find he's raising a flipping flag with his flipping crest
on it, so help me god—' and the footman looks

alarmed and knocks over a removal van with his paddle.

Later that day

Andrew barricaded himself in at Royal Lodge and threatened to give an interview to Emily Maitliss. We failed.

'The key to success,' said Clive, removing his headset, 'is to know when to stage a tactical retreat.'

11th July

7.30 a.m.

Charles is giving me a final run-through of his Christmas speech. He thinks he's going to stand up to deliver it, in a clear break from what his mother used to do. His theme is going to be rejoicing in the past, while embracing the future and ... he tails off and looks to Clive for inspiration.

'I know,' says Anne, who's dropped in to see the show. 'How about happy bloody Christmas, you nitwit, then a quick run through all the good stuff that's happened this year, draw a veil over everything else and don't mention the war. Or Harry and Meghan. Job done. Why do you have to make this look so effing difficult?' and she takes a drag of my ciggie, pulls some straw out of her hair and yells for her horse to be brought round.

Half an hour later Clive pokes his head round the

door, looking haunted. 'Has she gone yet?' he whispers.

10 a.m.

We're selecting the props. The late Queen used to have an ink stand and pen holder but Charles finds them triggering. 'I feel the same about dog bowls,' says William. He's come to supervise proceedings, or as he puts it 'make sure Pa doesn't fuck it up for the rest of us'.

'Language, darling boy,' says Charles mildly, and William punches a cushion and Charles says why?

'Just because, I suppose,' says William with a shrug. Anyway, what we need, we all agree, is a big happy family photo. 'Where are they all?' says Charles to no one in particular, glancing around the room.

'There aren't any,' says Clive, and we all ponder how odd that is, before realising that actually it isn't.

'Rats in a sack,' mutters Charles, and Clive suggests perhaps the solution to the props on the desk problem is to lose the desk?

11 a.m.

A keen new junior comms officer has joined us. 'I know,' she says brightly, 'we could take a photo of you, the Prince of Wales and the King, then just Photoshop everyone else in?' and Clive says yes, the press would never clock that one, it went entirely unnoticed when Kate fiddled about with a photo. Then he changes the subject. William says we're not using any pictures of his children because he wants them to have as normal a life as possible and behind him, I see Clive roll his eyes. The junior press officer says, 'But sir, didn't you once release a photograph of George, wearing tartan trousers, stirring a Christmas pudding, while standing on a box, in a palace, next to the late Queen? That's not an entirely normal upbringing, is it, sir?' And William glares at her and says that was different and Charles says 'She has a point, darling boy,' so William glares at him too and Clive stages an intervention. He says that Harry and Meghan are bombarding him with pictures of their children to put on the festive desk, along with ideas as to where exactly in the shot they should be.

'Let me guess,' I say, 'in the middle?' and Clive gives a ghost of a smile.

'They've sent professional to-scale drawings of the King's desk,' he says, 'with lighting suggestions, camera angles and names of directors, and' – and he makes quote marks in the air – 'all relevant agents and publicists, photo credit HRH The Duchess of Sussex, picture frame available to buy at www.americanrivieraorchard.com.'

'Do we think my darling Mama had agents and publicists gatecrashing her Christmas address?' asks Charles. 'Or flogging her photograph frames?' and Clive says it's doubtful, but he would very much like to have seen them try.

'What do you want me to do about the Sussexes?' he says. 'If I ignore them they'll go berserk and if I reply they'll go berserk on television.'

'Did somebody say television?' says Andrew, who's appeared in the doorway. 'I'm told I have a natural charisma in front of the camera. And what about a picture of me on the desk?'

'Who let him in?' says William, and we all stare at the cornice.

Later

'I'm very much a solutions chap,' says Andrew who's still here, because he always is, 'and I think the solution is me. Who's the one member of the family who hasn't been on the festive desk in recent years? Me! Who will the public therefore be crying out to see? Me! I could put on my velvet cap as well, if you like, or the full ceremonial dress for the rank of admiral which I commissioned for Papa's funeral but no one would let me wear it.'

The room falls silent as we consider the prospect of celebrating the birth of the baby Jesus with Andrew dressed as an admiral.

12th July

Another day, another York visitation. Today he was wearing a brand-new Savile Row suit, a shirt with a cutaway collar ('Suitably spivvy,' as Charles put it to me), handmade shoes and carrying a bucket with

'Donations welcome' on the side and a card reader clipped to the rim. 'Where did you get that?' Charles asks and Andrew says Fergie found it in a skip in Windsor and thought it might come in useful. We all fall silent once again, pondering the image of Fergie going through a skip in Windsor.

'I've got a lovely picture of me in my full garter robes, with a plumed hat and everything,' Andrew continues, oblivious to the silence, while behind him Clive grips the door frame with one hand and makes throat-cutting motions at me with the other.

'It's a lovely offer, but perhaps next year?' I say diplomatically. 'When the unfortunate ... um ... paedophile stuff has, um, faded ...?' and I tail off and Andrew puffs and goes puce and opens his mouth to say something.

'Tell me,' I say brightly, 'how are the blood prin-cesses?' and he looks gratified again and starts to tell me. He mentions that they'd very much like to do some royal duties as long as it isn't when they're on holiday or at Soho Farmhouse or having lunch in Chelsea. 'They'd be a real asset to the family,' he says, and without losing eye contact, I back slowly towards the window where the footman is waiting down below with the urn.

That evening

Andrew's gone off with his bucket and I'm watching *Below Deck Med* and talking to Annabel on the phone. Captain Sandy is getting stern with the younger members of the crew and the chef is having a melt-down because there's an unexpected vegan on board.

'Ridiculous way to live your life,' I mutter.

'Oh?' says Charles absently.

'Veganism,' I say. 'Waste of good cows.'

'I'm thinking bugger the lot of them,' says Charles and I look up, startled. He's never expressed an opinion on vegans before, and if he did I'd be inclined to think it was pro, not 'bugger' them.

'My speech,' he explains, 'the family photo we don't have. Bugger the lot of them. We'll use one of my original watercolours from my bestselling children's book *The Old Man of Lochnagar* instead.' I tell him that's a brilliant idea and make a mental note to order Clive to hide all the copies, and at the other end of the phone, Annabel overhears and starts to laugh.

13th July

Crisis talks with Clive first thing, about the props. I told him about Charles's *Old Man of Lochnagar* watercolour idea and he came closer to spluttering than I've ever seen before.

'But that's a wishy-washy sketch of an old man in tartan knickerbockers!' he says. 'It was published thirty years ago! For toddlers! Our motto for the new reign is forward thinking, while looking back with love. Or maybe it's backward thinking while looking forward with love. But whatever it is, it is NOT a fictional old man wearing tartan knickerbockers and looking out over a pastoral scene that's probably long since been turned into a Lidl.'

'Calm down, Clive,' I say, 'the tartan knickerbockers aren't happening and if Charles really puts his foot down then we tell him he can wear them himself. No one will see them if we crop him at the waist. And anyway,' I say, 'I've had a brilliant idea.'

'Oh?' he says.

'Yes,' I say. 'Corgis.'

'Corgis?' he says. 'Since when were Corgis anything but a terrible idea?'

'Not a patch on Jack Russells, I agree,' I tell him, 'but are there any left?'

'I think there might be, actually,' says Clive, 'we did a headcount of everything that moved after the late Queen died and I seem to remember there were two. They tried to make a dash for it but the footman laid an urn on the floor and they ran straight in. He clamped a silver salver over the end so we could tag them and then off they went. No idea where to, though.'

'Bally clever of the footman,' I say, 'Imagine being so good with dogs AND urns.'

'Thinking about it, they might be Dorgis,' Clive says, 'but it hardly matters as nobody apart from the late Queen can tell the difference anyway, can they?' and I tell him crossly yes, of course we can. Honestly, they could be donkeys and Clive wouldn't know. He comes from Devon. Possibly Cornwall. Savages.

'I know that the Corgis each have four paws and woof and belonged to the late Queen,' he says, 'and that's all I need to know,' and he goes off to find out more about their current whereabouts and availability as props for the Christmas speech.

14th July

I invite Charles and the comms woman in to hear what we've decided.

'Corgis,' I say to Charles, 'that would be a nice touch, don't you think? For your first Christmas address as monarch? A photograph of your mother's Corgis, and possibly one sitting peaceably at your feet.'

'Have you ever met a Corgi?' says Charles. 'Peaceable sitting isn't really what they do.'

'Fan-bloody-tastic,' mutters the comms woman, scribbling busily in a notebook. 'A link to the past, with a nod to the present, but embracing the future. *The Mail* couldn't put it better themselves. They probably won't even try.'

We all agree it's a marvellous idea, so brilliant that one could almost have Andrew to thank for it, and we laugh like drains at our joke.

15th July

'Ahem,' says Clive, walking in and looking sheepish. Charles and I look at him expectantly, but he looks at his feet and squares his shoulders and takes a deep breath. I nudge Charles. 'I'm fairly sure these are bad signs,' I whisper, as Bluebell and Beth sense the atmosphere and tense but Charles says not to worry, Clive always has everything under control. I feel in my pockets for ciggies just in case, open the window a crack and check for the footman. He gives me a wave and a thumbs up.

'So, the Corgis,' says Clive, 'or possibly Dorgis, it doesn't matter. The good news is that there are two of them, as we thought.'

'Well, that's bally marvellous,' I say, and Charles starts clearing a suitable space on his desk where the pen stand used to be.

'The bad news,' says Clive, 'is that Fergie has them,' and we turn pale, 'at Royal Lodge,' he continues, in the deathless hush we use for all things York, 'and the ducal flag of residence is flying.'

I'm the first to rally.

'Well,' I say briskly, 'it was a nice idea, but that's the end of that. No question of us asking the Yorks for a favour because they'll charge interest and demand a wing of Windsor Castle or a balcony at Royal Lodge for fly-pasts. Why don't we talk about horses instead of Corgis? Marvellous things. Proper tails. Much less likely to hump the dining-room chairs, and there's a lovely-looking filly running in the three-thirty at Newmarket.'

1st August
Balmoral

All the windows are open and the wind is howling round the castle.

'It is not freezing,' Charles tells me irritably, 'it is bracing. There's a difference.'

2nd August
Balmoral

'It is not freezing,' Charles tells William irritably, 'it is bracing. There's a difference.'

3rd August
Balmoral

'IT IS NOT FREEZING,' shouts Charles, as we assemble for dinner in coats, hats, scarves and gloves. 'How many times do I have to tell you all that?' William and Kate have flown up with the children on British Airways, overjoyed that this year they didn't have to fly El Cheapo from Luton to make Harry and Meghan look bad.

'Were those two really still here this time last year?' says Charles. 'I thought they were long gone by now,' and I explain again about the difficulty of making a three-part documentary on the back of ten minutes in the royal family. 'Ten minutes?' he says. 'As long as that? Time flies when you're having fun,' and we laugh. It's all still a bit tense though, because the Yorks are here and Fergie's started doing a podcast. The last time a royal did a podcast it didn't end well for anyone, especially her. 'Although to be fair,' I told Charles, 'Meghan can speak whole sentences which nobody understands. Fergie can at least make herself understood, we just wish that she couldn't.'

I was going to ask Charles what he thought about it all while we were dressing for dinner, but he was hanging upside down from the picture rail in his boxers. He says it's good for his spine, but it's difficult to have a conversation with someone auditioning to be a bat and besides, he was stressed. He'd made William drive Andrew to church and William was in a bait about it.

'Why me?' he said. 'Just so we all look like one big happy family and nobody mention the dead American paedophile?'

'Yes,' said Charles. Bluebell and Beth are on fine form, though, as long as you're not Clive's ankle in which case they're problematic, and there's always little Louis to lighten the atmosphere.

'We've been doing potato prints today, Granny Camilla,' he said earlier. 'Would you like some on your lovely white dress?'

5th August
The Highland Games, Braemar

'You've got competition today,' I say to the Hot Equerry with a friendly wink and he smooths his sporran and looks bashful. Anne's coming too. She's in a skirt which she bought in 1962 and describes as 'sturdy' and a hat that looks like a horse ate it.

'Good lord, Anne, it'd give Philip Treacy a hernia,' I tell her and we guffaw in a most un-royal way and Charles looks pained and says do you have to make such a noise? Anne and I look at each other and say 'Yes.' The Hot Equerry tells us it's time to go and Anne nudges me and whispers, 'Don't you love it when he orders us about?' and Charles looks exasperated and says, 'Girls, do at least try to behave,' and off we go. We have a family bet each year to see who can look like they're having the most fun in the photographs. 'Oh, that explains it,' said Annabel when I tell her. 'I've never understood it. Every year there's one of you on the front page looking like you're having the absolute time of your life, but you're actually sitting in the rain watching some bruiser in a skirt throw a tree trunk up a field. It all looks bally grim, if I'm honest.'

'Not when you've got a tenner on Edward coming last,' I told her, 'and evens on someone dropping the caber on Andrew's foot.'

The next three weeks

Still at Balmoral

All the windows are open and the wind is howling round the castle.

'It is not freezing,' Charles tells me, 'it is bracing . . .'

Back at work, or at least in London which might be the same thing. Busy week of activities. First we're en route to Liverpool to open a bridge, or possibly a bypass. Charles is grumpy because he doesn't approve of roads or bridges. He says we should walk everywhere, or cycle, because it's better for the environment. I consider pointing out that walking and cycling also generally require roads and bridges, but decide better not. Instead I say mildly, 'But we're in a car right now, darling. On a road,' and he says yes but that's different, just like it's different when William gets hot under the collar about climate change then flies from London to Norfolk in a helicopter.

'I mean, he could quite easily cycle there instead,' says Charles and I decide to let it go because he's now switched to talking about Poundbury, which always puts him in a good mood. He tells me that he's arranged for the street rental bikes in Poundbury to be penny farthings.

'They're beautiful, recycled, sustainable and wholly in keeping with my vision for modern life,' he says, staring happily out of the window and looking for trees to count, which he does on long journeys if he's feeling anxious. Then he frowns.

'Where are all the trees?' he says and I pat his knee and explain that we're on the North Circular but there'll be some trees shortly, and definitely by the time we get to Cheshire. He looks gratified and goes back to the penny farthings. They'd be perfectly adequate to get William to Norfolk, he says, and far less likely than a helicopter to plummet from the sky in a burning fireball, with catastrophic consequences for the line of succession.

'Very few trips by penny farthing end in a fireball,' I agree and he nods.

'But darling,' I say, 'penny farthings aren't always practical, at least not for everyone, in every situation. And besides, they're not exactly ten a penny,' and he looks suspiciously at me and asks if I'm making a joke and I say I wouldn't dream of it.

Somewhere on the M6 – two hours later

I'm reading my briefing notes for the Liverpool trip. They seem to have been prepared by Clive, which is normal, and our foreign policy expert, Sir David Manning, which is not. He used to be a senior diplomat at the Foreign Office.

'Why has a former senior diplomat from the Foreign Office written our briefing notes?' I ask Clive, who's looking mutinous on the jump seat. 'We're only going to Liverpool. It's the same country, isn't it?'

'Yes and no,' says Clive, handing me another sheaf of paper. 'When visiting Liverpool,' I read out loud, 'avoid mention of riots, Toxteth, scallies, scousers, whingeing, militant tendency, the *Sun*, Derek Hatton or Wayne Rooney's "Auld Granny" prostitute.'

I look up at Clive in astonishment. 'But what else is there?' I ask, and he says perhaps we could stick to the pleasantries like the weather, or the new rest area for the nursing staff. 'Rest area?' I say. 'Nurses? I thought we were opening a bypass?' and he mutters something about us giving him the coronary kind of bypass and Charles snaps, 'Speak up man, I can't hear you.'

'I said "yes and no",' says Clive, 'but mostly no. It's a new hospital, did we not explain that?' and Charles huffs and looks out of the window and asks where are all the bally trees in Birmingham.

'There don't seem to be any just yet,' I tell him, 'but oh look, darling, a horse-box – there might be a horse inside.'

2nd September

I call Annabel to touch base. 'We made it back from the former People's Republic of Liverpool,' I tell her, and behind me Charles says don't use that word and I say what? Liverpool? and he says no, republic. I shush him and go back to Annabel.

'Richard and Judy don't seem to be there any more,' I tell her. 'Terribly sad. Where have they gone? Do you think they're alright?' and Annabel says perhaps they've gone to Channel 4 and I say good point, we'd never see them on there. 'I don't think we even get Channel 4, do we?' I ask Clive and Annabel says we're bound to for the racing 'but they're a little bit ...' she pauses, 'meritocratic. A little bit ... republican.'

'Don't mention the R word,' I say and hang up.

9th September
Strictly Come Dancing launch night

'Best night of the year,' I tell Charles, ordering supper trays to be brought in at 7 p.m. sharp. 'And a bottle of the good stuff,' I tell the butler. 'Don't try to fob me off with that £10 zinfandel from M&S.' He looks at Charles, who's trying to economise, and who says that if I were blindfolded I wouldn't have a bally clue if it's red or white. 'Bally rude,' I told Annabel, 'and not even true. I have a very refined palate. I can tell instantly if it's gin or vodka.'

Tonight Charles shrugs and says he's drinking white anyway, a 2004 Burgundy is what he has in mind and the butler bows and goes out. The window's open and ready because it isn't completely freezing yet, and the footman has his orders. He's to stay in post for the next ninety minutes, never to desert it on pain of dismissal, because one can never tell when the excitement of launch night might get too much for me. He's been taking lessons from Penny Mordaunt in how to hold a heavy object upright for long periods of time. Charles once asked why it has to be an urn, why he couldn't just hold an ashtray, and I said have you ever tried dropping a cigarette butt into an ashtray from five feet up? and he said, 'Well no, when you put it like that.'

'Also,' I told him, 'Annabel says an urn is more queenly. An ashtray is a bit *Emmerdale*. She says as a general rule, if they sell something in OKA or Peter Jones, it's OK. If they don't, for example ashtrays, then it's not the done thing.' Charles mutters that not smoking at all might be more the done thing and I give him a quelling look and make a note to text Annabel and check that OKA really do sell urns and also who she thinks Johannes should be partnered with.

12th September

William calls to say that he and Kate are hiring a CEO.

'A what?' says Charles and William explains that it's a chief executive officer who will be everywhere, know everything, and report directly to them about what s/he knows, which will be everything. 'We already have one of those,' says Charles, 'we call him Clive. Can't recommend Clives highly enough. If you want to call yours by letters of the alphabet instead, then I expect it's just a generational thing.' William says the CEO will also have a name, and Charles says well as long as it isn't Clive that's fine, because two Clives would be very confusing for everyone. Not least Clive.

'One Clive could be seen as an accident,' says William drily, 'but two looks like carelessness,' and Charles says you should be so lucky. William says he's also been doing a headcount of all the staff and he thinks there are far too many middle managers and we might need to rationalise the workforce.

13th September

'Why did he keep talking about middle managers?' Charles asks me. 'Whatever can he mean? Are they some sort of mini-Clive? Trainee Clive?' I realise an answer's required but I'm knee-deep in the second *Bridgerton* book and reluctant to put it down. Annabel said the books are even better than the Netflix series, and she's right. 'Although that could be because it's the only bally Netflix programme we're allowed to watch round here,' I complained to her. 'Clive set parental controls on the juicy stuff that has either "crown" or "Harry and Meghan" in the title and even the Beckham fly-on-the-wall was banned because he said it might give me ideas about private jets and conspicuous consumption. Hopefully he doesn't know about the time I went partridge shooting in Spain on the Duke of Westminster's private jet.'

Tonight there's clearly going to be no more *Bridgerton* for me, as Charles wants to talk about middle managers. I clip my mini enamel Jack Russell bookmark on to the page and close the book.

'Aren't middle managers something to do with football?' he's saying. 'Do we have any football players on the payroll?' and I explain that no, middle managers are all the people underneath Clive, which is everyone except us, but not as far down as the gardener because Clive doesn't care about plants or ponds or anything that can't talk.

'Even horses and dogs?' I once asked him.

'Especially horses and dogs,' he replied.

'Strange man,' I say now, pondering this. 'But basically, darling, middle managers are people who use pens in their day-to-day jobs, and look nervous when Clive walks in. Yes, darling,' I say, as he opens his mouth to say something, 'I know you often look nervous too when Clive walks in, but that's different. Look, darling, a horse!' I say, changing the subject and pointing at the TV, where the Channel 4 racing is on.

Later I call William. 'Out of interest,' I say, 'how many middle managers is too many?'

'About 98 per cent of yours,' he says. 'I've sent some detailed suggestions to Clive,' and my heart sinks.

14th September

Quiet chat with Clive to discuss staffing levels. He arrives with a big red folder, a marker pen and a book called *Redundancy Protocol for Dummies* tucked under his arm. We begin with the junior staff, the people Charles once called The Essentials. 'That's the name of the own-brand towels at Peter Jones,' I tell him, and he looks blank. I realise he's never been to Peter Jones and doesn't know what it is. Clive calls the meeting to order and I say is that really necessary Clive? It's just you, me and Charles, and he consults his new book and says 'Yes'.

'Well,' I start, 'there's the urn footman of course,' and Clive raises an eyebrow the merest fraction.

'The urn footman?' he repeats.

'Yes,' I say, 'he's the footman who holds the urn.' Clive looks at me. 'You must have noticed,' I carry on, 'he's been here as long as I have.'

'Ma'am,' he says, and that's never a good sign, when he starts a sentence with 'ma'am', 'forgive me, but I find myself at something of a loss. Why is it necessary for a footman to hold an urn? And do you consider it to be a full-time job?'

'Well,' I say, giving the matter serious consideration and surreptitiously checking if the window's open because I suspect I'm going to need it, 'it depends. If I've given up smoking, which I very often have, then no, I'd have to say that it's probably not a full-time job and he could fit in a few other light chores as well.

One doesn't need an urn for a vape, you see,' I explain, 'or a nicotine patch,' and Clive starts to tap his fingers very slowly and quietly on the desk and I head for the window.

Five minutes later

'But,' I continue, 'if I AM smoking, which to be honest these days is more often than not because it's really quite stressful being Queen, well then yes it really is full time. Sorry. One simply never knows where and when the urge might strike, you see? And one must factor in the time it takes him to get from one window to the next, depending on which room I happen to be in.'

'Oh, one must,' says Clive, and I start to feel more confident in my defence of the urn footman.

'It's highly skilled work,' I say, 'and you wouldn't believe how big his shoe budget is. Awfully wearing on the soles, you see, running up and down gravel paths all day. And he needs quite a lot of physiotherapy, it puts great strain on the neck, all that looking up expectantly,' and Clive looks at me and I look at Charles, but he's looking out of the window and counting bally trees again, even though he knows perfectly well there are four through that window, five if you count the holly, which Alan Titchmarsh says is actually a bush and should in any case be dug up to make room for an acer.

'We're going to have to just tell him,' says Charles

decisively, without turning round. 'He doesn't know what the urn is for. The urn is an ashtray, Clive,' he says, turning round. 'My wife can't smoke inside, obviously, but nor can she stand around outside all the time like some bally barmaid. So the urn footman hurries round the outside of the building waiting for her to light up, so she can ash through the window and throw the butt out when she's finished, but without it spoiling the plants or littering the grounds.'

'Marvellous chap,' I say, 'couldn't manage without him. Oh look, a horse!' I cry, pointing at the television.

'That doesn't work with me,' says Clive, 'and besides, there isn't one. It's *Bargain Hunt*,' and he writes 'urn footman' in his notebook and puts a neat red line through it.

17th September
Sandringham

We're having a weekend shooting party and the animal rights people are kicking off online, which seems terrifically unreasonable of them.

'Pheasants are stupid animals,' I say to Charles. 'We're doing them a favour by shooting them and besides, as Annabel once said, they'll all get eaten in the end, in delicious pies and casseroles, so what more could they ask for?' Andrew's here, which is a bore, but when I asked Clive why he said 'because he always is and nobody seems to know how to make him not be'.

'Isn't that what you're for?' Charles asks Clive. 'To uninvite Andrew and make sure he isn't here? Or there? Or anywhere in between?'

'What could possibly go wrong, it's a perfectly straightforward shooting party?' I say, quoting Andrew in his wretched *Newsnight* interview.

'That is not funny,' says Charles, and Clive stares at the cornice.

21st September
Clarence House

Charles is working quietly through his boxes and I'm watching *Below Deck* with headphones on so I don't disturb him. In the distance I can hear Andrew banging on the front door.

'I know you're in there,' he shouts, 'drones don't lie, so stop pretending. A tenner, that's all I need for a roof over my head tonight and a hot meal.' He's started doing this as a forewarning of his tactics if we ever get him out of Royal Lodge. The footman knocks apologetically and asks what we'd like to do about *the situation*, as he delicately puts it, and Charles says he's been wondering that for sixty-three years. I sigh and pause *Below Deck*.

'Release the dogs,' I say and Bluebell and Beth hurtle

out the door barking furiously. Dimly I hear Andrew shouting 'Ow! Ow!' – and then silence.

24th September

Exciting day. The Household Cavalry are coming round for me to name their new drum horse and I've been brainstorming ideas with Annabel. 'I know, how about Kim?' she suggests.

'Kim?' I say. 'Whoever heard of a horse called Kim?'

'Kylie?' she offers. 'Khloe?'

'Oh god,' I say, enlightenment dawning. 'You've been watching old episodes of *The Kardashians* again, haven't you?' and she looks ashamed and says she can't help it and that love rat Tristram Thompson has been cheating on Khloe again, and Kylie's dramatic post-baby weight loss is a cause for concern and do I know that North West has done a new TikTok video making pasta? I gape at her.

'Stop,' I say, 'just stop. Stick to *Below Deck* like a normal person, or *Bridgerton* if it's been a bally tough day. The Household Cavalry do not need a Kardashian-themed horse. Now go, you're not helping.'

'How about Kris?' she shouts over her shoulder as I shoo her out of the room. 'You could tell them it's Chris after Sir Christopher Wren. Try it! They might like it!'

25th September

Andrew's broken in to tell us he's planning his seventieth birthday party.

'But your birthday isn't until February,' I say, 'and you aren't going to be seventy.'

'Exactly my point,' he says. 'These things take time and we need to pull out all the stops. Twenty-one gun salutes won't be enough.' Charles and I look at each other but don't bother interrupting because I surreptitiously press the panic button. Help is on the way.

'Celebrations will include,' says Andrew, reading from a piece of parchment that Fergie presumably found in a skip in Windsor, 'but not be limited to, a ball for nine hundred of my closest friends at Buckingham Palace—'

'Will any of them be paedophiles?' I ask and he glares at me.

'And a national service of thanksgiving for my seventy years at St Paul's.'

'But you're only going to be sixty-four,' says Charles.

'I know I'm going to be sixty-four,' says Andrew with exaggerated patience, 'I've been counting. Because I can,' and Charles makes polite noises of congratulation and looks at me and I signal to the footman at the window to be ready with the urn. 'With events this large,' says Andrew, 'detailed forward planning is essential.'

'A service of thanksgiving is usually held after

someone has died,' I say carefully, 'someone whom everybody loved and wishes to honour in death,' and Andrew looks gratified and says quite so.

'This is the genius of my idea,' he says, 'to hold it while I'm still alive, to hear all the lovely tributes!' Charles walks over to the window and says he has a sudden urgent need to count trees. Andrew looks around with that curious air he has about him, as if he's expecting a round of applause. The footman looks at me for guidance and I give him the nod.

'Time to go, sir,' he says, and takes Andrew by the arm. 'Wait!' Andrew cries. 'I'm only thinking small amounts of *foie gras* and caviar and why would Beyoncé not want to appear on the roof of Royal Lodge singing "Irreplaceable"? Brian May did it for Mama and he isn't even pretty. And the fountains in Trafalgar Square will run with claret for you lot,' he says, pointing at the footman and trying to shake him off. 'They'll love it, and me!' and in the distance I hear the front door slam. I ask Charles how many trees he counted and he says none at all, he had to close his eyes to cope, and I say I know how he feels and make a run for the window, which is already open.

30th September

We are off to Norfolk to open a fish shop. 'Will we be going anywhere near a bookies?' I ask the chauffeur. 'I want to put a tenner each way on Queen C in the two-forty-five at Sandown.' Clive says he's not sure me going into a bookies is quite the photo we're hoping for in tomorrow's papers. 'Oh what a pity,' I say briskly. 'What would you prefer? Charles with a cod on his head?' and Clive looks out of the window and starts counting to ten.

1st October

William's come over to complain about the photographs in the newspaper. 'Oh god,' I say to Charles, 'you didn't go near that cod when I had my back turned, did you?' and he says no, definitely not, he did exactly as Clive said. 'So what's the problem?' I ask William. 'It's not you, it's me—' he says wistfully, and I wonder if he's been watching too many rom-coms.

Apparently whenever there's a photograph of him and Kate in the papers, they crop him out and he's fed up with it. 'I mean, I'm going to be King one day,' he says petulantly, and I say oh, don't you start on about that, I've had years of hearing that. Charles looks peevish and William tries a different tack. 'Just because I'm a balding middle-aged man and Kate's an absolute showstopper in her prime, and incredibly photogenic—' and I say, 'Stop right there and think about what you've just said.'

'Oh,' says William and leaves.

7th October

We're at the British Racing School in Newmarket to open some new stalls. 'Have you got any going spare?' I say to the nice chap who's showing us round and he looks startled and says what? Stalls? And I say no, horses. 'I'm looking for something placid to hack around Wiltshire,' I tell him. 'Fifteen hands, Annabel says she's not fussed about the colourway as long as it goes with navy,' and the man looks confused and says his smallest and slowest is eighteen hands and goes like a rat up a drainpipe. 'Never mind,' I say, 'just bear it in mind for next time, there's a good chap,' and I cut the ribbon and give a carrot to the gelding inside the stall. 'Look, darling,' I say to Charles happily. 'A horse!'

9th October

Clive arrives looking despondent. 'Whassup?' I say cheerfully, because I've been watching too much *Below Deck*. Clive says Andrew's been in touch to say how much he's looking forward to seeing us all at Sandringham at Christmas.

'But he isn't invited,' I say.

'I know,' says Clive. 'But he's coming and he's bringing the whole family because he says it's what the late Queen's Corgis would want. And he's asking if the shooting party will be the bells and whistles variety or more straightforward and can he invite some of his friends?' and Charles and I shout 'NO' in unison and Clive says quite so.

14th October

To Chatsworth for the weekend. Me and darling Amanda, the Duchess, are reminiscing about the time one Easter when darling Debo, her late mother-in-law, put chicks in little boxes filled with straw in a line along the middle of the dining table.

'Such a charming centrepiece,' says Amanda with a sigh of admiration, 'such a talking point.' I move over to the window for a ciggie and wonder if the footmen here are well trained. 'Awfully clever of her,' I agree. 'I tried it myself once, but the dogs got them. Feathers everywhere. Absolute bally carnage,' and Amanda looks vaguely alarmed. I peer out for the footman and give him the thumbs up and in the distance Charles gallops past with the Duke.

'I don't suppose you've any horses going spare?' I ask her. 'About yay high, goes with navy?'

16th October

It's Charles's seventy-fifth birthday next month and Harry's been in touch. We knew he was going to call, because he issued a press release in advance saying so and asking for privacy. Charles puts him on speaker-phone. 'Yo, Pa,' he says, 'happy birthday. Can we come to Sandringham for Christmas?' and Charles looks at me, startled, and says to Harry, 'But why would you want to?'

'Because content is king,' says Harry, and Charles says, 'Actually, darling boy, I'm the King,' and Harry says no, he doesn't understand, 'content is king' is what the Netflix people say. It's stuff that fills airtime. 'And I'll cut to the chase,' he finishes, 'which is we need more of it. And if we came for Christmas, Meg and I could finally lay to rest the ghost of the Sandringham Summit,' he continues, 'when you were all beastly to us. Everyone said we weren't allowed to be royal, but without the boring bits, while also making lots of money on the side out of being royal. That adversely affected our mental health.'

'Mine too,' mutters Clive, and Charles says to Harry no, he can't come for Christmas.

'How about if we just bring a skeleton crew,' says Harry, 'just a couple of cameras, lighting, the producer, director, intimacy co-ordinator because, well, have you seen how hot my wife is?' and Charles looks helplessly at me and I look at the cornice and make a mental note to tell someone to dust it. 'Super-unobtrusive,' I hear Harry finishing. 'You'd never know the crew were there.' Charles rolls his eyes and hands the phone to Clive, whose finger hovers over 'end call'.

'And hardly anyone would have to bow or curtsey to Prince Archie and Princess Lilibet,' Harry carried on, 'only Edward, Sophie, their children, the Kents, the Gloucesters. And possibly Andrew should bow to them as well, just because. Not that we care. We barely notice these things. Get back to me on it, OK?' Then he says he must dash and shortly after a press release pings into Clive's Inbox. It announces that the Duke and Duchess of Sussex would have loved an invitation to spend Christmas at Sandringham with the rest of the royal family, but to their great sadness and regret it has not been forthcoming. It demands privacy at this difficult time and also copy approval. It ends, 'Hi-res images of the Duke and Duchess and their children Prince Archie and Princess Lilibet looking sad at the rejection, but also cute, are available on request for prominent front page use only.'

20th October
Windsor Castle

I'm chairing a meeting of the Sussex Survivors' Club (Windsor branch). Charles says it's best if he doesn't come, because surviving his own son won't sound very good if it gets out, and it's bound to. I'm in the chair and we're sitting in a circle sharing our stories.

One of the younger members asks if we should hold hands, but I give that idea bally short shrift. 'It's a symptom of the rot,' I say. 'Wherever you look, grownups holding hands like teenagers. Princes, prime ministers, they're all at it, I wouldn't even put it past the Archbishop of Canterbury. You never saw the late Queen and Prince Philip holding hands, did you? The last time Charles reached for my hand I put a riding crop in it. Thought he wanted to go for a hack. So anyway. No. We're supposed to be surviving the Sussexes, not copying them,' and she says yes ma'am, and I call the meeting to order and invite the first survivor to share.

'My name's Charlotte and I'm a 332 days' survivor,' says Charlotte. 'Hi, Charlotte,' we all say, and she starts to tell her story which involves fingers being snapped in her face and 4 a.m. emails demanding action by 7 a.m. and everyone nods sympathetically. Then a rather dashing chap in uniform stands up and says he's Tom, the Keeper of The Tower, and tells a story about the night the Sussexes banged on the gate in the early hours of the morning, demanding to be let in.

'I explained that we can't just open up for anyone at 5 a.m. and the Duchess said "It isn't just anyone, it's HRH The Duchess of Sussex, not that I care about the grandeur of titles. I've brought my hairdresser, he's just flown in from LA."

'So I said, "But why are you here now?"' Tom continues. 'And she looked at me incredulously on the intercom and said "Do you have no knowledge of the trans-Atlantic flight schedule at all? Like, zero?" and I said no, I don't, I'm the Keeper of The Tower and she stared at me and said, "Well, he's here and I'm here and what quite obviously is NOT here – yet – is a tiara. And he needs to practise doing my hair with it ahead of the wedding, like," and she snapped her fingers at the intercom screen, "Now",' and poor Tom is shredding a tissue in his hands as he speaks, and his voice starts to break and the group says 'Stay strong, Tom.'

'Cheer up,' I tell him when he's finished, 'she won't be banging on the door ever again,' and the meeting finishes with tea and biscuits and a group hug.

22nd October

The butler says the gardener wants to talk to me and I panic. 'Where's Charles?' I ask. 'He'd be far better off talking to him.' The butler says he's closeted with Clive and he doesn't want to disturb them. I sigh and shove the Tattersalls horse catalogue under a cushion so Charles won't know I've been shopping, and head out to the garden.

'What are your wishes with regard to this, ma'am?' says the gardener, sweeping his arm round what looks like the garden. 'Let me see now,' I say hesitantly, playing for time. 'Interesting question. Flowers?' and he says 'Excellent choice, ma'am, but it's a pond.' I say well, how about some fish then? and he says very good, ma'am, and over there? pointing towards something else green. 'Definitely flowers,' I say, 'or possibly trees and I must share my views on, um, shrubbery with you one day very soon, but not right now. But the grass is looking wonderful,' I say in desperation, and he looks gratified. 'It's a really excellent . . . um—' and I cast around for the right word but realise I have no descriptive words for grass. 'Length!' I say trium-phantly. 'It's a really excellent length,' and he says thank you ma'am, that means the world, and I suddenly feel out of my depth and panicky and in the distance I see the footman running towards me with the urn.

'Must dash,' I say to the gardener, and he bows.

Later

I tell Charles about my little chat with the gardener and how wonderfully clever he must be to understand about grass and shrubs and all those other things. He looks pleased. 'I told him to get some fish for the pond,' I say, 'and he seemed to think that was a good idea and best of all he didn't ask for any suggestions as to what sort. I wouldn't know a monkfish from a fish finger,' and Charles chuckles and then looks pensive.

'Sometimes,' he says, 'I wonder if a knighthood's good enough for lovely Alan Titchmarsh, seeing how very clever he is with my garden at Highgrove. I think actually Lord Titchmarsh of wherever he lives might be more appropriate. Shall we send him straight to the Lords?'

'I'm not sure that's in your power, darling,' I tell him, and he looks at me, astonished. 'Really?' he says. 'I'm sure we used to do it when that other fellow Fawcett was still here,' and Clive glides in and says perhaps there's a connection between that and the fact that Fawcett isn't here any more?

24th October

Charles and I are having a quiet night in going through the diary for next week.

'Monday,' he reads. 'You're going to a regenerative textiles exhibition in Carlisle. What on earth did you say to Clive to deserve that? I'm going to a reception to mark the thirtieth anniversary of Bees for Development. For heavens' sake, who writes this stuff?' he says irritably. 'Does that mean the bees are in favour of development? Or they need it themselves? Or that we should be bearing the bees in mind before we develop anything? Which,' he says, hitting his stride, 'is quite obviously what we should be doing. And did I tell you what we're doing about the bees in Poundbury? It's absolutely fascinating,' and I say yes, darling, I mean no, darling, I mean tell me again, darling, I never tire of hearing about your plans for the bees in Poundbury. He smiles fondly and says, 'I love you,' and I pat his hand and smile at him and we reminisce about having what Andrew and Fergie once called 'a marital moment'.

'They were doing it when we were all at Balmoral last year,' says Charles.

'I told them "Pass the sick bucket. Also, you're not married," and Fergie said no, but such a fine figure of a man, don't you think? and he has the most wonderful plumed hat. Anne made a very impolite retching noise, William had to leave the room suddenly and Louis said "Can I have a plumed hat when I grow up,

79

Mummy?" and Kate said "Shush darling, no, definitely not."'

'What's next on the agenda?' says Charles, changing the subject.

'King's Lynn,' I say. 'Both of us. Tuesday morning.'

'Why?' says Charles.

'That's a bally fair question,' I say absentmindedly,
scanning the itinerary of market stalls and local
produce and a new exhibition on coracles at the
county museum.

'To look delighted,' I say in the end. 'We're going to
King's Lynn to look delighted.'

27th October

Blessed night off from everything including darling
Charles, who turned out to be far too interested in
coracles in King's Lynn. 'Oh god,' I said to Clive in the
end, 'get him out of there, or he'll be placing an order
for ten thousand of them for every house in Poundbury,
or suggesting everyone in Birmingham commutes by
coracle along the canals.'

'Venice of the Midlands, Birmingham,' says Clive
and I stare at him, astonished.

'Have you been?' I ask. He looks at me as if I've lost
my mind and says, 'Of course not. Why would I have
been to Birmingham?'

Charles has gone to White's to do the King thing with William and I'm going undercover to a pop concert with Annabel, just like old times. The footman's put my Lizzo playlist on the Sonos to get us in the mood for dancing. The grandchildren tell me she's been cancelled but I said not at Clarence House, she hasn't, and I turn the volume up.

"'I was born like this, don't even gotta try",' I sing, putting my lippy on with one hand and waving my wine glass above my head. '"I'm like Chardonnay, get better over time".' Annabel arrives dressed in gold lamé and sensible shoes. 'I've been learning to twerk,' she says. 'Twerk?' I say, confused. 'Isn't that what we call that man from the BBC?'

'No,' she says, 'that's twerp,' and she leans forward, bends her knees, sticks her bottom out and waggles it. I look at her questioningly and she stands up.

81

'I'm not sure that's a good idea,' I say, 'you'll put your back out,' and she says perhaps I'm right. 'Is this Lizzo?' she asks, pointing to the Sonos, and I nod.

' "It ain't my fault that I'm out here making news",' I sing, dancing round the tasselled pouffe, ' "I'm the pudding in the proof, gotta blame it on my juice".'

'Goodness,' says Annabel, 'we *are* shaking our royal booty tonight, aren't we? Thank god Andrew isn't coming, you'd give him a heart attack,' and, clocking my horrified look, adds, 'Darling Andrew The Brig! Not Flagpole Andy!', and I shoot her a look of relief.

'You the baddest bitch,' I tell her affectionately, slipping on my special silver bunion-friendly dancing shoes and we link arms and head out to the Bentley, which is purring in the driveway.

4th November

Highgrove

A quiet night in. We're watching *Strictly* with our supper on a tray. I explained to Charles that we'd be having a TV dinner but he didn't understand. 'Where's the table?' he said, peering behind the door. 'Big thing, Georgian, mahogany, seats eighteen. I'd know it anywhere.'

'Don't worry,' I say, patting his arm reassuringly, 'it's still in the dining room where you left it, but I thought we'd try something more casual tonight as it's just you and me? We can get into our comfs.' He looks blank and I explain that I mean lounge suit instead of black tie, possibly even no tie at all, and no tiaras, not even a little one.

Charles looks dubious but he sits down and says we can have a debrief of how our day went, while Dianne's dancing. Her pink hair makes him anxious. He says it's a sign that we're out of kilter with the natural world. He can never settle until the camera pans over to Motsi, who has a calming but energising effect on him. I once asked him why and he said it's something to do with her figure, then he went cross-eyed and said 'Hubba hubba'. 'Maybe it's her feet,' he said vaguely. 'Very nimble. Lovely eyes, too.' The footman arrives bang on time with our dinner on two trays and I slice the top neatly off Charles's first boiled egg. He looks at it and winces, so I pass it to the footman, who underarms it smoothly through the window, from where there's a muffled 'Ow', and we move on to the second.

'You were talking about Poundbury the other day, and your vision for modern life,' I remind him, because he still seems upset about Motsi and needs soothing. 'Remind me: apart from penny farthings and organic oatcakes for all, what IS that vision, my fondest, cleverest love?'

'Well,' he says, looking gratified and gesturing to the under-footman to move the tray so he can stand up and do his King thing. 'I suppose it's a sort of *Trumpton* meets *Camberwick Green*,' and I smile encouragingly, 'where Mummy bakes a homemade

cake for when the children get home from school,'
he says, his voice rising, 'and Daddy does something
wholesome but lucrative, and everybody,' and he
reaches a crescendo and jabs a finger at poor Dianne,
who's doing the samba, 'everybody has natural-
coloured hair. Like yours,' he says fondly and I
think of the hours and hours I spend in the hair
salon getting bleach and tint tipped over it, and
decide not to mention that. 'Women look so much
better when they're natural,' he says, gazing at me.
Fortunately just then the camera pans over to Motsi
for her verdict. 'Hubba hubba,' says Charles and
sits down.

'I could murder a G&T,' I say to no one in particular and outside I hear the sound of an urn smashing as
the footman drops it hastily, and footsteps running in
the direction of the kitchen.

6th November

Top secret planning meeting for the annual Order of
the Garter ceremony next year.

'I vote that we just cancel it,' says William. Charles
says that's out of the question, the populace demands
it. William stares at him and says Pa, the populace
hasn't demanded a garter ceremony since 1472, and
who on earth uses the word populace anyway?

'Me,' says Charles.

'Someone who addresses the French National
Assembly as "*Citoyens*",' mutters Clive.

'Moving on,' I say sharply.

'More to the point,' says William, raising his voice so as to be heard above the bickering, 'if we have a garter ceremony, Andrew will insist on coming and giving it the full velvet-robed "Do you know who I am?" treatment. And if we all want the monarchy to survive – and I'm assuming we do because it's considerably better than the alternative, at least for us – then the best possible response to that scenario is "better not".'

The room's quite stuffy and I find myself nodding off. Just then Andrew abseils through the window wearing a velvet robe and a plumed hat. 'Can I help?' he asks, brushing himself off and stroking his feather. 'I don't wish to brag, but I'm something of an expert on garter ceremonies,' and Charles put his head in his hands. Just when I think it can't get any worse, Fergie starts banging on the door demanding a marital moment with the plumed hat and Bluebell starts humping the table leg. 'OFF!' I bellow and Andrew jumps and says don't you dare talk to me like that, I'm a prince of the blood and you're a jumped-up housewife from Wiltshire, and Charles punches him and the meeting descends into chaos. I wake up with a start.

8th November

Charles has summoned the royal stamp collection for a viewing and I try valiantly to pretend that I'm interested.

'It's the most valuable in the world,' he says, 'must be worth hundreds of millions.' I perk up.

'Are we selling it?' I say brightly. 'Pointless things, darling, stamps. You can't wear them, they don't sparkle and besides, nobody writes letters any more.'

'I do,' he says, 'to government ministers. All the time. Pages and pages covered in my signature black scrawl. They love it. They tell me they find them most interesting.'

'No, Your Majesty, we do not write letters to the government,' interjects Clive smoothly. 'That was then, before you were King. This is now. No letters, not even short, legible ones. No public opinions on architecture, up to and including the correct home for the Parthenon Sculptures. On which subject,' he continues, 'I have pretended that I didn't notice you wearing a tie covered in Greek flags at a particularly ticklish political moment for the sculptures last year, and you will humour me by never, ever doing that again. And definitely no future mention of herbal medicines, badger culls or the plight of the Patagonian tooth fish. Now you are King, your piscine interests no longer extend beyond UK territorial waters.'

'I think,' I tell him admiringly, 'that is the longest speech you've ever given,' but Charles looks mutinous and starts to talk about how endangered the Patagonian tooth fish is and I change the subject back to the surprisingly valuable £100 million stamp collection to lighten the mood. Or at least mine.

'You can get an awful lot of tiaras for a hundred mill,' I tell Charles with a wink. 'So important to keep the monarchy relevant by refreshing the jewels, don't you think?' and he chuckles.

'You and your bling,' he says fondly. 'Go on then, but just a little one, mind? No more than twenty carats all in,' and I try for a blush and look coquettishly up at him through my eyelashes and he blanches as he does whenever anything reminds him of Diana.

'Don't do that,' he says. 'Don't ever look at me like that.'

9th November

Charles and I are brainstorming holiday ideas for next year and he's suggesting Transylvania. 'Don't be ridiculous,' I say. 'Do I look like the sort of gel who goes to Transylvania?' He says he has no idea, how can one tell? I say well, as a general rule, if a country doesn't look like it sells Elnett, I don't want to go there.

'Nothing I have ever heard about Transylvania,' I add, 'gives me any confidence in the Elnett situation.'

'What have you heard about Transylvania?' he asks.

'Nothing,' I say. 'See what I mean? No confidence.'

'How about Romania?' he says hopefully, and I shake my head.

'Bulgaria?' he tries. 'There are some tremendously interesting early medieval monasteries in Bulgaria.'

I look at my husband, whom I love very much, and

consider the prospect of spending my valuable free time in an early medieval monastery in Bulgaria. I decide it's time for a more direct approach. 'You'll be suggesting Albania next,' I tell him, 'and god knows what other godforsaken places ending in A. Whatever next? Australia? Canada?'

Charles says don't be ridiculous, of course he wouldn't suggest Australia, there's no early medieval anything in Australia, let alone monasteries.

'I was thinking more France,' I say, 'specifically Paris, and even more specifically the royal suite at the George V. I hear the jewellery shops in the Place Vendôme are quite something. Annabel tells me that they have to be seen and visited one-by-one to be believed. And did you see that article in *Heat* about French pharmacies?' and he looks at me.

'*Heat* magazine?' he says blankly.

'No,' I say, nodding, 'realistically you didn't see it. But they're gold mines, French pharmacies, bally gold mines for a gel like me. Who knows what novel brands of extra-strong hair lacquer those crafty Frogs are hiding from me?'

12th November

Total panic stations. Harry and Meghan have announced they're coming over for peace talks.

'Wonderful!' says Charles.

'Why?' says Clive.

'Who asked them?' says William, looking

murderous. The footman has lined up dog bowls along the wall for him, and he's walking along methodically kicking them one-by-one and muttering 'Ow' under his breath.

'Dear lord,' says Clive, 'make it go away.' He says H&M are due to land later today and they've sent a list of preconditions, although how you can impose preconditions on a meeting you've demanded, with people who aren't going, is beyond him. Our comms woman explains that it's because Netflix will be film- ing their prep for the meeting we're not going to, and helping them to write the preconditions we won't agree to, because if something's worth doing it's only when the cameras are rolling. Clive gives me a know- ing side-eye and says, 'Thank you, Charlotte, that was most helpful,' and she blushes.

'We could just pretend to be out,' I say, but Clive shakes his head and says that won't work.

'You're right,' I say. 'Bluebell and Beth will start barking the minute they land. They'll smell them.'

'Really?' says Clive incredulously. 'Your dogs' sense of smell is so acute they can smell Harry and Meghan all the way from RAF Northolt?'

'No,' I tell him, 'but the footman's in the Sussex Survivors' Club. He had a terrible time, poor chap, green tea all hours of the day and night, avocados not quite ripe enough, and as he said, what's a chap from Uxbridge supposed to know about avocados anyway? Monstrous things, avocados, did you know? Poison- ous to horses. Anyway, to get his own back, he's been training the dogs with one of Harry's old sweaters and a hat Meghan used to throw at him. So now, whenever they get the faintest whiff of Sussex, they go ape, as my grandchildren would say.'

Clive gapes most impolitely.

'Don't gape, Clive,' I tell him mildly, 'it's most undignified.'

'Let me be clear,' he says when he's recovered his composure. 'Your footman has trained your dogs to set upon your family?' I sigh and put down *Country Life* and peer sharply at him over my reading glasses.

'Not MY family,' I tell him, 'not strictly speaking MY family. Only by marriage. His family,' and I point at Charles. 'But OK, hands up, yes. I'm trying to give up the ciggies, so I've been vaping a lot and using the patches, which means I haven't needed the urn so much, and the footman was bored. One thing led to another and here we are. And it turns out he's awfully talented with the dogs. They never paid me a blind bit of notice when I tried to wean them off your ankles,' and I go back to *Country Life* and Bluebell trots in and I bellow 'OFF' and Clive jumps.

14th November

Hours until H&M arrive: 12

The footmen are closing all the curtains and turning the lights off and we're hunkered down reading the preconditions list with a torch. It's headed 'Requirements in advance of a meeting held for everyone to apologise for everything or else we go on *Oprah* and it won't be pretty'. They have a way with words, don't they? says Clive, and reads on.

1. Netflix access all areas.
2. You will have no aides present.
3. We will have our lawyers, publicists, strategists, public relations consultants and Oprah.

Also Meghan's hair and make-up artist, stylist and milliner.

'Milliner?' I say to Clive. 'Why on earth is she bringing a milliner?'

'To see if the hat can be repaired,' he says. 'The one she kept throwing at the footman, which he used to train your dogs. Remember?' and he gives a brittle, bitter smile which is most unlike him. Charles says we should all go to bed and it will look better in the morning and Clive says he doubts that very much, but bows and retreats, shooting a warning glare in the direction of Beth.

'I saw that,' I tell him.

'Just joking, ma'am!' he replies. I go to bed feeling anxious.

Later that night

Clive is wearing a headset and looking at a screen with little red dots moving over it.

'That looks a lot like air traffic control,' I say, 'but it

can't be, surely? Because you're not an air traffic controller.'

'You'd be surprised,' says Clive, his eyes never leaving the screen. 'They're on their way from Northolt in a helicopter. I reckon we've got ten minutes.'

Charles looks sombre and gives the order to the butler to lower the flag and bar the door. It starts with polite knocking, which rapidly becomes louder. 'We know you're in there,' shouts Harry. 'Where's my hat!' shouts Meghan.

'I'm getting *déjà vu*,' I say to Charles. 'Didn't Andrew used to do this?' Bluebell and Beth are hurling themselves against the door so I shut them in the next room just as the door bursts open and Harry and Meghan walk in. '

'Surprise!' they shout. 'Not really,' says Clive, and I scream and wake up with a start. 'Darling one, you were having a nightmare,' says Charles, 'and more to the point, Harry and Meghan have been on *Oprah* to say they're not coming.'

15th November

Ray Mill House

Anne pops in on her way home from Costco. We knew it was her when there was a screech of brakes and a spray of gravel spattered against the downstairs windows. She roared up to the front door in her new car, a ten-year-old diesel Golf, belching fumes. It's just like my own darling Golf, which I call Ginny. 'Bally brilliant little runaround!' says Anne, getting out and banging the roof cheerfully, setting off the dogs who are inside. 'Why didn't you tell me about these cars before? All anyone round here ever talks about is bally Bentleys and Range Rovers and you can't bomb round Gloucestershire in one of those. Far too big. What you need is something German and solid,' she says, banging the roof and setting off the dogs again. 'I'm thinking of calling her Angela, as in Merkel. Bally good, no? Don't tell Charles. He kept asking why I couldn't just get a smaller horse, or a penny farthing or a bigger dog. I do sometimes worry about him you know. I said I can't do the bally Costco shop on a Newfoundland, can I?'

16th November

Time to start Christmas present planning

'What do you need me for?' asks Charles and I tell him that only he knows for sure who is a much-loved

93

member of the family and therefore getting a Christmas present, and who is not. He says do we have to keep using that phrase about much-loved? And I say yes, because if we stop they'll assume they aren't and then all hell will break loose. He nods sadly and mutters about rats in a sack. If he gets the much-loved present list wrong, I explain, there'll be at the very least a diplomatic incident and at worst a sit-down on *Good Morning America*.

I've got a list of everyone I think we might have to buy for in front of me, and Clive has drawn up a list of all the departments at Peter Jones where the presents might come from, along with an up-to-date store map and current location of the Emma Bridgewater mugs. He did try to suggest that Peter Jones might not be the only source of Christmas presents, but I assume he was just tired. 'There's the White Company across the road,' I concede, 'but one really doesn't need to bother because even the scented candle selection in Peter Jones is excellent these days. And apart from the White Company, where do you have in mind? And please don't say Harrods. We don't mention Harrods round here. Bad memories.'

That afternoon

'So the present list is drawn up in order of importance to the household,' I tell Charles and he brightens. 'So it starts with me!' he says. 'Splendid, I'm definitely a much-loved member of the family. What are you going to buy me?'

'Ah,' I say, 'no. I meant Clive. It starts with him.' Charles looks startled but rallies quickly and says what are we getting Clive, then? I say I was thinking some Acqua di Parma and Charles says he didn't know Clive was a keen swimmer. There's a puzzled silence.

'Swimmer?' I say.

'Yes,' he says. 'Acqua di Parma, isn't that some kind of up-to-the-minute goggles?' I say no, it's a bally expensive aftershave and Charles looks relieved and jokes whatever next, budgie smugglers? I laugh and tell him that as long as Clive doesn't start wearing Dior Eau Sauvage, like he does, we can buy him whatever we like 'Because we wouldn't want me snogging the wrong man by accident, would we?' There's another silence, more tense this time, as we contemplate the horror of what I've just said. I put a tick next to Clive's name on the list and we carry on.

'Does he have a wife?' I ask Charles.

'No idea,' he says, 'never asked. Let's assume not. It's better that way, at least for us'— 'which is all that counts,' I say, finishing the sentence for him and we beam fondly at each other.

Next day

'Right-o, we're nearly finished,' I say. 'We haven't discussed Harry and Meghan because I thought you wouldn't want to, but FYI I've already bought their presents.'

'Oh?' says Charles. 'What?' I explain that it's a pair of those talking fish you put on the wall, but bespoke. Annabel found them on Etsy, two for £19.99. The late Queen used to love her Billy the Bass which sang *Rule Britannia*. 'I've gone one better,' I tell Charles, 'I've commissioned a cod which says "You are much-loved members of the family" in your mother's voice. Genius, no?'

'And the second one?' asks Charles.

'It's a companion piece to the cod,' I say, 'a turbot saying "Recollections may vary" in William's voice, then the sound of a dog bowl being smashed.'

As we're getting ready for bed, Charles asks what I'd like for Christmas, and adds that it doesn't even have to be from Peter Jones. I tell him, 'Oh darling, I already have everything I could ever wish for,' and I stroke his knee affectionately, 'but if you absolutely insist—' and I gesture to the bedside table, where the book about the Crown Jewels is open at the aquamarine tiara. 'Matches my eyes,' I say, and he chuckles and turns out the light.

18th November

Battersea Dogs Home

Wonderful day off work, so I went shopping for a new dog. Bluebell and Beth are acting like they own the place and need some competition. 'Do they do horses as well?' I ask the Hot Equerry, who's coming with us but in a suit, not a sporran, for safety reasons. He says he thinks horses might be beyond Battersea's remit, 'But for you, ma'am, who knows?' I blush and Charles looks reproachfully at me and says 'Ignore her'.

'Do you do horses?' I say to the nice woman who greets us, 'because I could do with a new one for hacking round Wiltshire, fifteen hands, nice chestnut that goes with the furniture, what do you think?' and she says she's terribly sorry but it's cats and dogs only. 'I can be flexible on size,' I add, 'it doesn't have to be fifteen hands.' She looks apologetic and says strictly dogs or cats only, they can't even run to a tortoise or a hamster. Not to worry, I tell her, we'll get the horse somewhere else then, and the Hot Equerry jots 'get horse' in his notebook and underlines it neatly. Lovely chap. Terribly handsome. Battersea have lined up a few possibilities in the yard in order of size, from a Chihuahua to a grizzly bear, which is sitting placidly on its enormous haunches and drooling.

'Is that a grizzly bear?' says Charles, looking startled, and his protection officer hurls himself between him and the bear as a precaution.

'No,' says the nice woman, 'it's a Newfoundland. He's very friendly.' The protection officer dusts himself off and looks dubious. The Chihuahua's no good, I tell her, because while Bluebell and Beth are in general friendly, loving dogs, albeit occasionally boisterous, if there's anything smaller than them, or Clive's ankle, or cushions, or miscellaneous family members to whom they've taken a violent and irrational dislike then they tend to savage it. 'And that,' I tell the nice lady sadly, 'would probably include passing Chihuahuas.' She looks sympathetic and says of course, she quite understands. The Newfoundland has ambled amiably over to Charles and deposited a column of drool on his best Savile Row, and the Hot Equerry is beside himself.

'What's he called?' I ask the nice woman. 'Who?' she says. 'The King?' and I say no, he's called Charles, I know that. The dog, the Newf. What's he called? She says Bear. Bear lies down and looks soppily at the protection officer, who gives him a cautious stroke, and even the Hot Equerry looks a bit smitten.

'We'll take him,' I say. 'Even Bluebell and Beth can't bully a bear, but at least they might give poor Clive's ankles a break.'

20th November

'What are we doing today?' asks Charles, who's doing his bat thing and hanging from the picture rail. I check the diary. 'Opening a warship,' I say and he falls off with a thud. 'Ow,' he says, and I pause the Elnett mid-wing and glance over. 'Everything alright, darling?' I say. 'No. Actually make that NO. My darling wife,' he says, now sitting on the floor rubbing his head, with Bear drooling onto his lap, 'one does not OPEN a bally warship.' I pause again mid-spray and look at him in the mirror. 'You're turning puce,' I say.

'I know,' he says, 'it's the effect you have on me

when you talk about opening warships. One LAUNCHES a warship,' and I say well, my father was in the Army and my first husband was in the Army as well. How should I know anything about the bally Navy? He glares at me, because he hates it when I mention the Brig, but he's upside down again so it doesn't have the same effect and I carry on regardless.

'If there's anything you want to know about Sandhurst, I'm your gel,' I say, and he mutters something about me knowing far too much about bally Sandhurst back in the day, and all the men in it. I ignore him, and pick up the Elnett again.

'Sandhurst, yes. Parade grounds, yes. Dartmouth Naval College, and what one does with a warship, no. Bally marvellous uniforms, though, those Navy chaps. I don't suppose your equerry has a few of those at the back of the wardrobe that he's saving for special occasions?' and Charles closes his eyes and crosses himself upside down and says, 'Holy Mary Mother of God, give me strength.'

'Bit of a Catholic whiff about that, darling,' I warn. 'Careful, now. Remember what happened the last time a king did that,' and I give my hair a final enthusiastic burst of Elnett and there's another thud. 'Ow,' he says, and Bear licks his face.

It's bally freezing, I complain to Charles – why are all the windows wide open in bally December? He says it's a fresh sea breeze to blow the cobwebs away, even though there aren't any cobwebs. That's what staff are for, except for the urn footman. He's got nothing to do with any cobwebs, he's got a full-time job already. 'We must do our bit to combat climate change,' continues Charles, 'because Rishi Sunak has scrapped his climate pledges and says we can still buy petrol cars until 2035. It's an absolute bally disgrace.'

'But darling,' I say, 'you've never bought a car in your life, how do you know what they run on? That's what staff are for. And I still have Ginny—'

'Who?' he says.

'Ginny,' I say, 'my lovely old diesel Golf that I use to run around when I'm at Ray Mill, pop to Waitrose for gin and reminisce about the old days when they used to pelt me with bread rolls for upsetting Diana.'

101

Charles harrumphs, though whether it's the mention of Diana or diesel is hard to tell. 'Anyway,' I say, 'I'm not swapping Ginny for a horse and cart any time soon,' and Charles harrumphs again and I say but anyway, about the temperature in here? But he's gazing out of the window counting trees and ignoring me. I consider having an argument but remember the aquamarine tiara and put on a hat instead. It's a big Philip Treacy hat, sort of *Laughing Cavalier* meets *My Fair Lady*. It's a bit odd when it's just the two of us at home, together, but it does the job of keeping in heat. 'Bit much for breakfast,' says Charles mildly, but I shrug and say needs must, pull on my fingerless gloves and start methodically slicing the top off his boiled eggs. Charles peers at the eggs one by one and gives a running commentary. 'No ... no ... maybe ... no ... yes!' ... and so the day begins.

3rd December

Sandringham

Chef has been in to discuss food arrangements for the Christmas Eve dinner. There'll be thirty-four people, all of them relations, some of whom we like, plus seventeen dogs, two Dachshunds (do they count as dogs? I wondered aloud and Chef said well they definitely weren't cats, so let's assume so) and a rabbit.

'About the rabbit,' says Chef. 'Do we have any further details? Size, particular partialities?'

Well, I say, it belongs to Louis and he refuses to leave it at home. Chef looks worried.

'I'm not being funny,' he says, 'but is it a real rabbit that needs feeding? Or a stuffed one? I'm just planning the catering, not the entertainment.'

'Currently real, may be stuffed later if it doesn't behave,' I joke, and Chef stares at me and says nothing.

'So the rabbit will be wanting carrots,' he says finally. 'And the Dachshunds will be wanting —'

'The sweepings off the kitchen floor,' I say firmly. 'No idea who they belong to, certainly not me. Pointless dogs. Might as well put a pheasant on a lead,' and Chef stares at me and looks more worried.

'And the seventeen dogs?' he says.

'Ah yes,' I say with more enthusiasm. 'They're mostly Jack Russells so they get the fillet steak. There's a smattering of Corgis, or possibly Dorgis. Nobody's entirely sure, since the old Queen died, but never mind. Give them the rump steak. There's a couple of spaniels, but the proper working kind who pick up dead pheasants so we don't have to, not the pointless sort of spaniel which runs amok in Fulham.' Chef says quite so ma'am, he'll feed the spaniels a nice bit of rabbit culled on the estate. I'm enjoying myself now, so we discuss in more detail the exact nutritional requirements of small working dogs, non-working Jack Russells and Corgis/Dorgis, with particular reference to the weather forecast, any individual dietary requirements or allergies and the wishes of the late

Queen. 'Also,' I say, 'Clive says there's a worrying band of Westies moving in from the south, like a weather front.'

'Oh dear,' says Chef. 'Royal Lodge? I heard they'd got some new dogs to keep the Corgis company.'

'We fear so,' I say, and Chef nods darkly and says he'll rig up a flagpole in the kennels and lay in plenty of Pedigree Chum. 'Thank you,' I tell him, 'that will be all.'

'But ma'am, we haven't discussed what the people are eating over Christmas,' says Chef, 'just the dogs.'

'Oh, who cares,' I say, waving a hand airily and reaching for the Crown Jewels book, 'just shove a chicken in the Aga and hope for the best. Everyone loves a roast, don't they?' and Chef bows, and departs.

4th December

I'm starting the day as usual by reading the entries written in my work diary by my assistant. Today it reads 'Christmas Day outfit discussion with stylist'.

'Stylist?' says Annabel, reading over my shoulder with a bacon sandwich in one hand and a Bloody Mary in the other. 'D'you mean me? You don't have a bally stylist. That's why you wear the same thing every day. Coat dress, zip up the front, fit-and-flare, perky little hat that doesn't cast shade on your face, except when that hat chap's gone all *Laughing Cavalier*. And no,' she says, catching sight of my reproving expression at her taking Philip Treacy's name in vain, 'don't even think about giving it the full Queen. I'm your sister.'

'How could I forget?' I say with an attempt at wryness which only makes her laugh. 'And have we got the new OKA catalogue yet? Darling Fiona at Bowood says there are some lovely occasional tables and the pouffes are to die for. I thought if I banked them steeply enough against the windows it might keep out the draughts. My feet are like blocks of ice.'

Annabel considers the situation. 'Or you could just get some more dogs,' she says. 'Bank them round your feet like sandbags and you won't feel a thing. Bluebell and Beth would love the company and it might stop them humping Clive's ankle.' At my feet, Bluebell opens one eye and looks at Annabel witheringly, and Beth growls quietly in her sleep.

10th December

'Vintage year for Middletons,' says Charles amiably, hanging upside down by his ankles from the four-poster bed. 'Can't remember the last time I saw so many of them in one place. Do we know them all? Have we met any of them before?'

'Well,' I say, 'one of them is your daughter-in-law, Kate.'

'Catherine,' says Charles automatically. 'She wants to be called Catherine.'

'Whatever,' I say, 'only by them,' and I wave in the direction of the outside world.

'Do you know,' I tell him, 'when we saw the Macrons on the state visit, darling Bridge told me they find it all terribly confusing in France and call her Catherine-Kate,' and we hoot with laughter and Charles nearly falls off his perch. I don't tell him that Bridge also said 'And which of you gets ze pick of ze tiaras? And 'ave you seen ze one with the aquamarine slabs?' and I told her yes, I've very much seen the one with the aquamarine slabs and I have big plans for it.

'Anyway, there's also Kate's parents,' I tell Charles, reading from the guest list and bending over to look him in the eye because he's still upside down, 'her sister, brother-in-law, brother, sister-in-law, nephews, nieces, au pair, other nieces, some bally nice gels from I think New Zealand, who help with the chores, seven dogs, some of whom we know, four of whom we like, three hamsters, twelve tennis rackets and a netball team. Oh, and Louis's rabbit. And I think Kate's Uncle Gary might be here somewhere about the place but Clive dealt with him.'

'How?' says Charles.

'Best not to know,' I say briskly, 'deniability and all that. But I hear the pontoon moored a mile off Holkham beach is delightfully bracing at this time of year.'

'And the netball team?' says Charles, flexing his ankles cautiously.

'Fair question,' I say. 'Frightfully active family, the Middletons. Frightfully fit. Tennis, netball, you can never tell how the mood might take them, so they travel prepared in case they get restless.' Charles grunts and drops to the floor and the Newfoundland licks his face.

12th December

Charles and I are in the blue saloon having a light three-course afternoon tea. *The Archers* is on in the background because I tell Charles it's very important for him to know what's concerning his subjects. He says he's not sure a fictional programme on the wireless about a quaint rural village is the best way to tap into the travails of modern life, any more than *Below Deck Med* is an accurate portrait of everyday life on the ocean waves, but I give him a quelling look. Just then Clive walks in hurriedly, which is unusual, shuts the door firmly, which is alarming, and looks grave, which only happens at times of great turmoil.

'Has somebody died?' I ask. 'Andrew, for preference.' Clive says no, it's worse than that, or better, depending on whether or not you're Andrew.

'It's Louis's rabbit,' he says. 'It's on the loose.'

'Oh god,' I say. 'Lock down the house, nobody in or out, nobody moves, and do a headcount of the dogs.' Clive bows and hurries out to see to it.

'Out of interest,' says Charles, 'where are Bluebell and Beth?' and I blanch. Nothing would interest Bluebell and Beth more than a stray rabbit, not even Clive's ankle. Not even their favourite Chinese Chippendale back at Clarence House. I look at my lap, but it's empty. They're not on my feet, or under the sofa and they definitely weren't clinging to any part of Clive when he walked out because he'd have mentioned it.

'Gone,' I say balefully to Charles. 'They're gone.'

An hour later

Clive is in the kitchen interrogating Chef about dinner plans. 'So no rabbits have come in or out all day?' he says, and Chef shakes his head. 'No rabbit is on the menu and none of the sous-chefs could have gone off-piste and put it on instead of chicken?' and Chef shakes his head and says nothing happens in his kitchen without his say-so and nobody would dare skin a rabbit without asking him.

'And what are you feeding the dogs?' persists Clive, and Chef turns white and runs to the kennels.

Later

Louis's rabbit has been found, albeit lightly chewed around the edges and deeply traumatised, poor thing. It was being chased with some success by Bluebell and Beth but the urn footman saved the day. He found a giant Victorian butterfly net in one of the glasshouses, and staged an intervention, swiping the rabbit up from under their noses when he saw them pelting across the lawn in hot pursuit. The rabbit has a bandaged leg, but we've told Louis he's been to bunny hospital and will be fine by morning. 'Or at least not in a pie,' I mutter darkly to Charles as we get ready for bed. 'And make sure nobody reads that child *The Tale of the Flopsy Bunnies* any time soon.'

Christmas Eve

So we're in our bedroom getting ready for dinner and the big night. The royal family give their presents out on Christmas Eve which I've always thought is odd. 'The clue is in the name, Christmas Eve,' I told Charles when I was first invited to Sandringham. Not very long ago, come to think of it, and now I'm running the show. How times change. 'It's the eve of everything happening. Like turkey and presents.' Charles says well technically it's the eve of the birth of Christ and nothing to do with turkey or presents, and I wave my hand airily and say whatever. He frowns and stands up and hooks his thumb in his suit pocket and I say, 'Stop right there, Charles. We are NOT going to have the King thing in the bedroom, on Christmas Eve.' He sits down again and mutters something about being the head of the Church of England so he knows a thing or two about when Jesus was born. I close my eyes, think of the aquamarine tiara and let it lie.

The presents were a great success. We gave William a model helicopter because Charles says that's the closest he's going to get to the real thing now he's the heir. 'And look on the bright side,' he told him, 'at least it isn't a copy of *Budgie the Little Helicopter*.' He and

William had a terrible row about the helicopter thing months ago, because William said did he have any idea how long it took to get a wife, three children, assorted dogs and Louis's rabbit from Windsor to Norfolk at weekends? Clive looked at Charles and unfurled a roll of parchment, almost as if they'd planned this. It had the line of succession drawn neatly on it with a quill and a big fat arrow in pink highlighter pen pointing to King Harry and Queen Meghan, and their heirs Archie and Lilibet, if anything happens to William and his entire family.

'If, for example,' said Clive, 'to pluck one possible scenario from the air, you were all involved in a catastrophic helicopter accident and plummet from the sky in a fireball.' William said, 'When you put it like that,' and walked out. Clive says, 'Technically it should read Prince Archie and Princess Lilibet,' and I roll my eyes and say, 'Are we bovvered?', because I've been watching old Harry Enfield sketches with Annabel and Clive says maybe not, but they are. 'My point exactly,' I say.

Early Christmas Day morning

I'm flicking through the Tattersalls catalogue looking at the yearlings and Charles is watching a programme about Poundbury because it helps with his blood pressure. Alan Titchmarsh provided the voiceover and he's saying, 'The astonishingly benevolent and far-sighted vision of the Prince of Wales,' as the camera pans down the street, 'is why these fortunate people live in such a bucolic place.' We cut to a perfect family playing tennis in the garden and drinking homemade lemonade. 'Oh look,' I say, 'it's the Middletons! Where's Uncle Gary?' and Charles chuckles and says I'm terribly naughty and just then we're interrupted by a ghastly noise.

'Why is the telephone making such a bally odd noise?' says Charles. 'Why isn't it ringing, like it usually does? And why isn't anybody answering it, like they usually do?' I explain that it's actually someone FaceTime-ing us on the iPad and Charles looks baffled and I rummage under the cushions trying to find it. When I pick it up I freeze.

'It's Harry and Meghan,' I say, looking at the screen, and Charles looks around, panicked. 'Where?' he says. 'Under the cushions?' and I say no, they're on the iPad and I show him the Sussexes looking expectantly at their screen 8,000 miles away and waiting for us to answer. 'Can they see us?' says Charles, backing away towards the door with his hands up. I explain that no, they can't, but the call will stop soon if we don't answer, and they'll disappear from the screen, and go straight to a TV studio to complain we're ignoring them. 'Oh god,' he wails, 'what do we do?' but the call ends and there's a stunned silence.

'Good morning Your Majesties and a very happy Christmas to you both!' says Clive, walking in for his morning briefing and clocking our faces. 'Is anything wrong?'

'Yes,' says Charles. 'Very.'

'Out of interest,' I say, 'do you ever get a day off?'

'No,' says Clive. I consider this.

'It's probably for the best,' I say, 'at least for us. Happy Christmas,' and we tell him about the iPad incident. Clive says we must tell William and see what he thinks. Charles says it'll be unprintable, and Clive says well, that's fine because it won't be going into print will it? Charles stares at him and says he wishes he could be so sure.

Ten minutes later

William arrives, out of breath. 'Where are they?' he says, pelting into the room with Bluebell and Beth hard on his heels, because wherever William is, a dog bowl is never far away and it might contain treats. 'I knew they'd try it on at Christmas, the sneaky bastards,' and he starts shadow boxing round a Regency gilt torchère. Clive flinches. Charles tells William to calm down, they're still halfway round the world and still much-loved members of the family, depending on what day it is and who's asking. William looks both relieved and disappointed, and rubs his knuckles as if they're already sore from thumping someone. 'Why are they calling anyway?' he asks. 'What do they want from us?'

'Well, let's see now,' I say. 'Money? Fame by association? Titles? Private pet names for future children?' and Charles looks wounded and says maybe his darling boy just wanted to say happy Christmas and we all look at him to see if he's serious and realise that he is. I put my arm round him comfortingly.

'And tiaras,' I say, to break the silence, 'they might want tiaras, too, if we happen to have any lying around. And anything belonging to Diana which could be a talking point on breakfast TV ... do you know,' I say, because the silence is becoming oppressive and William's looking at me in the way he does if I mention his mother, 'it's the damnedest thing, but an old sweater of Diana's with a sheep on it sold in America recently for a million dollars?'

'How interesting,' says William, flexing his fingers. 'Who sold it? And did they live in Montecito?'

26th December

We're all gathered in the hallway after breakfast, about to head out for the Boxing Day shoot.

'Nobody,' says Clive, 'I repeat, NOBODY,' and he looks at Andrew, 'is to describe this, even in private, even without moving their lips, as a perfectly straightforward shoot. Do I make myself crystal clear?' and we all nod. Andrew puffs up in that extraordinary way he does, and looks as if he might be about to say something, or pop, and Clive quells him with a single glance. He partially subsides. 'I repeat,' says Clive softly, 'do I make myself clear?' and we all nod and Andrew pouts and Bluebell growls at him. 'Off, Bluebell,' I say quietly, so we don't cause a scene and out we go to wreak some jolly pleasant carnage on the pheasants. Stupid birds. Best thing for them.

'Get the raised game pie tin out,' I told Chef this morning. 'You'll be needing it.'

2nd January
Clarence House

'I'm back at work,' I tell Annabel, who's come round for a festive debrief bearing a new diary with 'Living My Best Life' stamped on it. 'Work?' she says. 'What are you talking about, work? You've never done a day's work in your life,' and I say that's not fair at all. I used to be a deb, which was no walk in the park. Cocktail after cocktail, even when you didn't fancy one. After that I was married to The Brig for twenty-odd years, and if managing him wasn't a full-time job then I don't know what is. 'I suppose so,' says Annabel grudgingly, 'although goodness knows you had enough help from all those other women eager to manage him too,' and I give her a withering look and a hard poke on the arm.

'And only yesterday I had to spend hours selecting the jewellery for the next state visit,' I continue, bringing my CV bang up to date. 'Later today darling Bruce is coming about some new ballgowns, and the woman

115

who makes the fit-and-flare coat dresses is coming tomorrow with swatches for the next batch.'

'Why doesn't she make them all reversible and save herself the trouble?' says Annabel. 'Two coats for the price of one. No one would know. Or you could get her to design something bally ELSE for once? And by the way, you are getting worryingly low on gin.'

'And,' I tell her, stung that she thinks I might be under-employed, stuck in a fashion rut or lacking in gin, 'Chef is coming to discuss seasonal menus involving pheasant. When was the last time anyone asked you for a considered view on a pheasant? I've had to spend bally hours watching that nice Hugh Fearnley-Whittingstall grow beetroot and joint dead animals on YouTube, so Chef doesn't think I'm stupid.'

Annabel concedes that it is indeed a very long time since anyone pressed her on pheasants, if ever. 'I mean, one just shoves a chicken in the Aga and hopes for the best, really, doesn't one?' she says. We nod companionably and agree that's really all one can do with a chicken, hope for the best, and I feel a pang for my Aga at Ray Mill.

'I wonder if I took the Bolognese out of the bottom oven when we were there before Christmas?' I wonder aloud.

3rd January

Annabel FaceTimes from Ray Mill. She's just got the Bolognese out of the bottom oven, three weeks after it went in. 'Think of it as well marinated,' she says cheerfully, scraping a blackened crust off the top and feeding it to the dogs. 'It's perfectly alright underneath,' she says, peering at the rest and poking it with a wooden spoon. 'Nothing wrong with it at all. I'll batch it up for you and put it in the freezer. Cheerio!' The screen goes blank and I turn to Clive, who's come for a briefing about the week ahead. He's trying to look as if he fully expected our conversation to be dominated by a burnt Bolognese 85 miles away. I give him a reassuring double thumbs up, he raises one eyebrow and on we go.

4th January
Clarence House

It's Clive's deputy, Chris, in charge today and he looks nervous. Clive's at a management training meeting all day, he explains. I stare at him. 'Someone's trying to train Clive?' I say. 'Goodness, whatever next.' Chris says it's a new directive from someone high up. 'Who high up?' I ask. 'The King?' and he says no, he thinks it might be someone in human resources and we agree that it's all most odd because what have HR got to do with running anything?

'Who even are they?' I ask Chris. 'Where do they live? It can't be Wiltshire because I'd know them,' and Chris says he doesn't know but he can find out. I say on second thoughts no, it's best not to know. I suspect it's south of the river, because that would explain a lot, and we turn instead to the day's schedule.

Later that day

Charles walks in and I pause *Below Deck* and mention the HR incident and how odd the whole thing is. 'Why do we have them?' I ask. 'Things used to run perfectly well before we had an HR department.'

'Meghan didn't think so,' he says darkly and I drop the remote control in alarm at him unexpectedly using the M word. 'She said we needed an HR department, so we hired one and now we can't sack them. HR rules. Clive says the only thing HR departments can do is get bigger and bigger until eventually they employ us all, rather than the other way round.'

'And then what happens?' I ask.

'They sack us all,' he says. I consider this for a moment, and think of Ray Mill and the burnt Bolognese and happy days doing nothing. I sigh and press play on *Below Deck*.

5th January

After his last day of training, Clive pops in on his way home. 'Home?' says Charles. 'I assumed you lived here, being a bachelor.' Clive says actually he has a wife, and a life, and they live in Clapham, just over the river. Charles gapes and says, 'Wife? Life?' I gape and say, 'Clapham?' Clive looks sheepish and starts talking about the training. 'I now know that it's very important to get a diversity of opinion from a representative sample of the royal household before we decide anything,' he says. Charles looks impassively at him and says, 'But the only opinions which count are ours.'

'Quite so,' says Clive, 'but they've told me and I've told you and now we can safely ignore them. Although you might like to bear in mind that the urn footman has the right to request a transfer to other duties, if he wishes.'

'Why on earth would he wish to?' I ask. 'What more could an urn footman want than to hold an urn?' which is a compelling point if I say so myself. Clive obviously thinks so too because he doesn't press the issue.

6th January
New Year trouble at Royal Lodge (1)

Someone from HR told Andrew that if he wanted to retain a full household staff he'd have to go for management training and learn how to do it properly. He called Charles in a fury.

'Management training?' he shouted, 'I am a magnificent manager of men!' Charles said he believed women as well as men could now hold senior positions in the workplace and Andrew snorted in derision. 'You only have to *look* at me to know how magnificent I am as a manager of men,' he said. I was in Her Late Majesty's Royal Navy for twenty-two years, managing countless men.'

'I thought you were mostly flying a helicopter,' said Charles, 'on your own.' Andrew said that was only some of the time. It was the more heroic part of the job, when he risked life and limb for his country while developing a curious inability to sweat. Had he mentioned that before? Charles said yes, and he was hoping he'd never mention it again, perhaps especially not on national television.

'There was lots of less heroic stuff you don't know about,' Andrew went on. 'I'd describe it as noble work more than heroic. Vitally important to the national interest. As is everything I have done in life.' Charles made a mildly strangulated noise and asked where this diverting run through ancient history was leading us. 'Not to a bloody management training course in Slough,' shouted Andrew and Charles asked if perhaps one solution to the problem of the training course was not to have a full household of staff? That retaining 257 people and a full-time Corgi groomer to cater to the needs of two unemployed pensioners might not be strictly necessary? 'I am Queen Elizabeth's son and the Corgis are her dogs,' said Andrew, 'and shame on you for forgetting that.' Charles said, 'Are you by any chance wearing your garter robes right now?' and Andrew said what if he was? Then he slammed the phone down so hard Charles's pens rattled.

'That went well,' I said, and turned up the volume on *Below Deck Med*.

7th January
Trouble at Royal Lodge (2)

HR called Fergie and said she needed to reapply for her job.

'What job?' she told them. 'I haven't got a job.'

'Exactly my point,' said the woman from HR.

8th January
Trouble at Royal Lodge (3)

' "When sorrows come, they come not single spies, but in battalions",' murmurs Charles, and sighs. He has a tendency to quote from Shakespeare when the going gets tough. 'Don't tell me,' I say to Clive, 'someone from HR called Andrew and said the Corgis need to retrain as poodles and they have just the course in Slough?'

'Not quite,' says Clive carefully, 'but in response to a question about diversity Andrew pointed at Fergie and said "She's a woman!" Someone else phoned Beatrice and Eugenie and asked them whether being a blood princess is a full-time job and whether some specialist training might help them reach their full potential.' I hear someone snort and glance up in surprise, then I realise it's me. I disguise it as a cough and peer out of the window in the hope of locating the footman.

'And?' says Charles, ignoring me. 'What happened next?'

'Several things,' says Clive. 'Fergie asked what potential meant and if Americans might be interested in buying it if she packages it up in a nice biscuit tin with a crown on it. Eugenie asked if fulfilling her potential would be time-consuming because she is, and I quote, a busy working mother. And Beatrice said she thought it would prove an interesting topic of conversation next time anyone at, for example, *Vogue*, asks for an interview about her life as a modern princess. Her exact words were "It would be good to look like fresh, modern princesses, in touch with the national mood." There really was an interview in *Vogue* a couple of years back,' he adds, 'and the staff member who thought that was a good idea has now been dealt with.'

'Would you care to expand on that?' I ask, looking at him over my glasses.

'No,' says Clive. 'Anyway, back at Royal Lodge, after Andrew had proved to HR his diversity in the form of Fergie, I'm told that the footman arrived with afternoon tea and scones and Andrew told Fergie he was thinking of commissioning a new flag.' Charles puts his head in his hands and I accidentally drop the burning match out of the window and there's a faint smell of singeing when it lands in the footman's wig.

9th January

Andrew's been summoned to see his brother. He's looking mutinous.

'What's she doing here?' he says and Charles goes puce and says how dare you question the presence of my wife? And at least she's my wife, not my ex-wife, unlike some people round here . . .

'Not Camilla, the dog,' says Andrew, 'Bluebell. She's always trying to hump something. It's embarrassing, and Fergie says it's disrespectful to the late Queen.'

'She'd know all about that,' I mutter into the pages of *Country Life* and Andrew says did you say something? No, I say, don't mind me, you boys get on with things.

'About this new flag,' Charles says firmly.

'How do you know about that?' says Andrew, and Charles says never mind how he knows, he doesn't think a new flag is a good idea. It won't look good if it gets out, and it's bound to, and how much is it costing anyway?

'No need to worry about that,' says Andrew, 'an old friend of mine from Kazakhstan is covering the full cost, plus a bit more because he says it's a privilege to be my friend. You can see why, can't you?' He's looking in the mirror. Clive starts to twitch. 'It's all entirely above board,' continues Andrew, 'and besides, my flagpoles and friends are nothing whatsoever to do with you.'

The room falls silent. Clive stops tapping his fingers on the mantelpiece. Charles looks at Andrew and Andrew starts to inflate in that peculiar way, and looks defiantly at Charles.

'Everything is to do with me,' says Charles, 'but most especially your friends, your finances and, may god help us all and grant me patience, your flagpoles.'

Andrew goes puce. At my feet, Bluebell starts to quiver.

'It's not just a new flag,' he blusters, 'it's about keeping the old craft skills alive. I'd have thought it's right up your street? Without me the whole heritage flag-making industry would be unemployed.'

'Shall I take this one, sir?' asks Clive and Charles nods.

'Making flags is not an old craft skill,' Clive tells Andrew. 'It is sewing. Sewing is in no danger of dying out, ergo flags are in no danger of dying out. You will cancel the order and there will be no new flag.'

'I hate it when you use long words like "ergo",' says Andrew mulishly, 'and what about the flagpole? I've commissioned a new one of those, because hardly anyone makes those any more. In fact if it wasn't for me, that skill would—' Clive raises his palm at Andrew to tell him to stop and Bluebell starts to growl softly. It seems appropriate in the circumstances, so I don't tell her to stop. Charles tells the footman to see Andrew out, and Andrew says forget it, he's going anyway. Beth shoots off my lap and I consider saying

'OFF!', but my heart isn't in it. Instead we all watch as Andrew tries to leave the room with a semblance of dignity, while trying to shake a small, cross, determined dog off the hem of his trousers.

'That was surprisingly enjoyable,' I say to Charles. 'Perhaps we should invite him over more often?'

10th January
Trouble at Gatcombe Park

Clive says that Anne's been on the phone complaining about HR. She was driving at the time, so the conversation was conducted against a background noise of harrowing gear changes and enthusiastic swearing.

'What training course do they want her to go on?' says Charles. 'Speed awareness and blasphemy?' Clive says they never got round to that because Anne arrived at the stables and said she found them more interesting than Clive, and rang off without saying goodbye. Clive wondered if Charles could put in a good word with her about how useful the HR department is, and what sterling work they're putting in with Andrew. Perhaps he could persuade Anne, when HR call her, to be less . . . and he paused to find the right word. 'Combative?' Charles looks at him.

'You want me to tell Anne to be less combative?' he says, with an air of disbelief. 'Have you met my sister?'

12th January

Lunch at Bentley's with the Brig, who arrives with a spring in his step and a glint in his eye.

'You're up to no good,' I say, kissing him fondly on both cheeks. 'I know that glint of old.'

'I'm on Hinge,' he says.

'Hinge?' I say. 'Oh dear, has your arthritis flared up? Or is it a new pill for your blood pressure?' but he shakes his head and looks smug. 'Oh gawd,' I say, 'it isn't another name for Viagra, is it? Because if so, I don't want to know. I'm the Queen now, you know,' I tell him with a twinkle in my eye. He says no, it's a dating app and the children set it all up for him. They put a picture of him with all the dogs around him, an old one of him in his Army uniform 'for context', nothing to do with the fact that he looked bally hot in his Blues and Royals get-up, and a picture of his favourite horse, 'because you can tell a lot about a chap from his horse,' he finishes and I nod. Wise words. He says there are so many ladies on there keen to meet him that it could quite go to a chap's head. He's taking one of them for cocktails at Duke's later. 'Absolute corker from Majorca,' he says.

'Majorca?' I say. 'Really? How odd, what's wrong with Wiltshire?' and he says she isn't really from Majorca.

'What on earth are you talking about?' I say exasperatedly. 'Where's she from then?'

'Bayswater,' he says equably, 'but it sounds funny, doesn't it? A corker from Majorca,' and we both chortle and he orders half a bottle of champers and a dozen oysters to start.

'Oysters, darling?' I say. 'Are you sure that's wise?' He winks at me and says he's positive and we have a lovely jolly lunch talking about the old days when we were married. We hardly saw each other because we were both so busy seeing other people, but it was all terribly good, innocent, highly sexed fun.

'Hunting, shooting, shagging,' he said happily leaning back with his drink, 'just like a Jilly Cooper novel.'

'You are terribly naughty,' I tell him fondly as we leave four hours later, 'and absolutely incorrigible.' He says he knows, but it suits him, doesn't it, kisses me on both cheeks, doffs his trilby and saunters away up Piccadilly in the direction of St James's. I get into the Bentley which is purring gently by the kerb and say, 'Home, James, and don't spare the horses!' as I always do. Is he really called James? Annabel once asked, and I said no of course not, he's called Colin, why d'you ask?

15th January
Bowood House

Time for our monthly book club and this month we've been reading *Spare*. I'm giving a lift out to Bowood to Helen, our new recruit. She's terribly jolly, I picked her up at the WI in Kensington. We were both having a sneaky ciggie round the back and she was checking the odds on the four-forty-five at Epsom. 'We're a tight-knit bunch,' I tell her in the back of the Bentley as we purr down the A3. 'Just Emma, Amanda, Annabel and Fiona, who owns it.'

'Owns what?' she said.

'The house,' I say. 'Bowood,' and she says isn't Bowood a stately home? I think about it for a minute and say well, it's a house and it's quite big, but isn't everybody's? Helen says yes of course but also not really, and looks worried. 'It's all terribly informal,' I say, to put her at her ease, 'just us and 40,000 square feet of Palladian architecture set in rolling parkland. Now, what did you think of *Spare*?' and she says she thinks Harry is an ungrateful little toad and I tell her we're going to get along brilliantly.

Bowood – noon

The butler greets us in a morning suit, all very informal, and shows us into the blue saloon, where the gels are kicking things off with a cheeky glass of champers.

'Champers?' says Fiona, waving to a footman carrying a silver salver of glasses. He hurries over on cue. 'The wonderful thing about Bowood,' I say to Helen as we both take a glass, 'is that the footmen are terrifically well trained, if you know what I mean.' She looks alarmed and says no, she has absolutely no idea what I mean but she's a happily married woman. I take her elbow and guide her to the window, which is open just the right amount, and point out the footman standing underneath, holding an urn and looking expectant. See? I say. Helen looks blank.

'Is he looking for the gardener?' she asks, peering down. 'Or planting tulips?'

'Neither,' I say. 'The urn. We ash into it.' Helen looks at the footman and looks at me and says 'Righto!' and sparks up. Kindred spirit, Helen.

Clarence House – that evening

When I get back from Bowood, the hall smells faintly of Eau Sauvage. I ask the butler when Charles got home and where he is and the butler says about 5 p.m. but he got the sense that all was not well. Just then, Clive glides in so smoothly I sometimes wonder if he's on castors. I asked him once, actually. I said, 'Clive, do you have wheels instead of feet?' and he said, 'No, ma'am, but I expect it can be arranged if you would like.'

'I'm afraid Fergie's been here,' he says now, 'asking for money.'

'Well, we're used to that,' I say brightly. 'Happens all the time. Nothing we can't deal with, surely? Beth and Bluebell must have been around the place somewhere, they know the drill,' and Clive says no, this time was different.

'She brought the Corgis,' he says, 'or possibly Dorgis. So hard to tell. She said they can't even afford Cesar any more, soon they'll have no choice but to feed them Pedigree Chum and is that what the late Queen would have wanted? She said the shame and dishonour are too much to bear.' I sigh and kick off my shoes and a footman runs to pick them up but I say no, not to worry, you focus on the urn, I'll take care of the shoes myself. Clive carries on talking as we walk to the drawing room. 'Then Andrew called,' he continues, 'and told Charles it was grossly disrespectful mostly to him, but also to their mother's memory, to allow tinned dog food at Royal Lodge.'

What did Charles say, I ask Clive. 'Are the shades of Pemberley to be thus polluted with Pedigree Chum?' I laugh out loud. 'I don't suppose Andrew thought it was funny, did he?' I say, and Clive says no. Andrew said 'What? Who lives at Pemberley? Is it bigger than Royal Lodge? Does it have a flagpole?' Charles said never mind, it's Jane Austen and Andrew said he doesn't recall meeting her, because he was at Pizza Express. By this point poor darling Charles was positively drooping in his chair and Fergie was making herself at home, issuing orders about what she'd like for dinner. 'Bea and Euge are coming too,' she told the staff, 'they're hungry too. It's not just the dogs.'

'Well, what did the dogs used to eat before you fell on hard times?' Charles asked Andrew in the end, and Andrew said 'fillet steak'.

'What a coincidence,' I say, 'that's his and Fergie's favourite.'

'A happy coincidence, ma'am,' says Clive, and I wink at him.

'Their butler told our butler that their favourite TV supper was tournedos Rossini,' I say, 'fillet steak with *foie gras* on the top. Charles went bananas because he thinks *foie gras* is cruel, although,' I say *sotto voce* so Charles can't hear, 'they're bally nasty birds, geese. Arguably best thing for them. Not much better than pheasants.' Anyway, Andrew asked how was he supposed to proclaim his status when eating a TV dinner at home with his ex-wife, if not by putting *foie gras* on his steak? 'What would you have me do?' he added. 'Eat sirloin?' Charles said no of course not, don't be ridiculous, but Andrew had already hung up and Fergie had her feet up on the sofa and was calling her daughters telling them, 'Come over, I'm at Clarence House.' Clive had to be firm with her until she left.

As we get to Charles's study we pass the Hot Equerry on his way out who's looking upbeat. 'I think we're over the worst,' he says. 'We spent some time with a picture book about Poundbury which seemed to do the trick and now he's giving his pens the once-over, which always calms him. Over to you, ma'am.' Clive and I look at each other and go in.

Charles is sitting in his favourite armchair, with his pens laid out on a red velvet tray next to him, watching a fly-on-the-wall called *Inside The Tower of London*. He looks up when I walk in, smiles fondly and points at the TV. 'It looks surprisingly comfortable these days,' he says. 'Even the really damp and chilly bits down by the river have Wi-Fi. Let's not rule it out for the much-loved members from Royal Lodge and Montecito, eh?' Clive and I exchange relieved glances and Clive bows and departs.

22nd January
Gatcombe Park

Comparing notes on the new HR department with Anne. She's drinking tea out of a chipped mug, feet up on the coffee table, watching an old video of the Horse of the Year Show in a VHS machine. 'Don't tell me,' I say, 'Fergie found it in a skip?' She snorts and says not a chance, it's never left the house since it arrived, marvellous bit of tech.

'HOYS 1998,' she adds cheerfully, picking dried mud off her jodhpurs. 'Vintage year. Fiftieth anniversary. Have a seat.' Commander Tim wanders in and says darling, your boots, the mud, the coffee table. Anne licks her finger, rubs a spot on her left boot, peers at it and says, 'Clean as a whistle!' Tim shrugs and says, 'More tea, dear?' and Anne says she'd bally love some. What time is it, she shouts after him. Too early to add a tot of something cheeky?

'Never too early,' I say.

'Righto!' shouts Commander Tim and Anne calls Zara to tell her she must find HOYS 1998 on YouTube, or come over to watch it on the VHS. Tim comes back with three mugs of tea and hands one to Anne, who sniffs it appreciatively. 'Chin chin!' she says and we all clink mugs.

'So,' I say, 'Charles is wondering how you've been getting along with our new HR department?' Anne shrugs and says they haven't given her any flak since she told them she doesn't employ any staff in the house. 'Unlike some people I could mention, particularly those with flagpoles, I'm not bally made of money,' she told them. 'I have limited resources and no friends in Kazakhstan, so I prioritise horses, not humans. Never occurred to them to ask how many people work in the stables. Dozens and dozens and dozens of them. Countless numbers, wonderful boys and girls the lot of them. So I think I'm in the clear.' We high-five and clink mugs again and I ask Commander Tim if he can make mine a bit stronger next time. 'Let your hand slip, whoops! with the bottle,' says Anne, miming tipping it upside down. 'Easily done,' I say equably, 'happens to me all the time. Damn slippery things, bottles. Shall we watch 1999 after this? And oh, just look at those horses!'

25th January

The comms woman arrives for the daily briefing. 'It's the Duke of York's birthday next month, on 19th February,' she says. 'Will we be wishing him many happy returns on our social media accounts, as we do with other members of the family?' I look over at

Charles and he looks out of the window and sticks a finger in both ears and hums, 'Rum pum pum diddly um pum pum.'

I sigh and turn back to the comms woman.

'I'd take that as a "No",' I tell her and she puts a line through 'Duke of York birthday' on her clipboard. 'And the twenty-one-gun salute at The Tower?' she asks, and Charles and I gape at her most un-royally. 'What twenty-one-gun salute?' says Charles, with a dangerous edge to his tone that is not lost on the poor comms woman.

'The one Andrew says it would be appropriate to do,' she says, 'just after the other eighteen-gun salute in Hyde Park?' she adds, trailing off and looking uncomfortable. 'I take it he made that bit up, then, did he?' Charles and I nod and she curtsies and leaves.

1st February
Ray Mill House

Going over options for the book club with my assistant. I'm in my green tweed Wiltshire mufti, which Charles once said makes me look like Bagpuss. 'But Bagpuss is pink,' I protested, 'and a cat.' Charles looked at me adoringly and said, 'Saggy old baggy old cloth cat, a bit loose at the seams, but Charles loved her.' I said oh darling, you old romantic, and leaned in for a kiss but then Clive walked in and looked utterly appalled and the moment passed.

'So,' says my assistant, dragging me out of my daydream, 'you asked me to edit the original options down to three. So we've got rid of the new Jilly Cooper, an old Salman Rushdie and something by Sebastian Faulks that wasn't *Birdsong*.'

'So what are we whittled down to now?' I ask.

'*Charles III* by Robert Hardman, *Charles at Seventy* by Robert Jobson, *The Prince of Wales* by Jonathan Dimbleby and *Prince Charles: the Passions and*

Paradoxes of an Improbable Life, by Sally Bedell Smith.'

'Hmm,' I say, 'so tricky. Are we quite sure those have universal appeal? It's not just me in the book group after all,' and she says absolutely, no question about it, His Majesty is endlessly interesting and anyone would be privileged to read any one of these books. I look at her doubtfully and wonder if we've hired a sycophant or someone who used to work for Andrew, which amounts to the same thing. Then she says she's put a wild card entry into the mix, Jilly Cooper's *Riders*. 'That's the one,' I say. 'Pop into Amazon and ask them to deliver copies to all the gels.' She says we don't pop into Amazon and I say no, I suppose not, what do we do? Call? Charles would probably write them a letter.

2nd February

A letter arrives from the man himself, who's just up the road at Highgrove with a surfeit of footmen. They've got nothing to do except deliver letters, because at Ray Mill I have an ashtray, not an urn. Bliss. I open the letter.

'Your Majesty, my darling wife,' he writes in his black spidery scrawl, 'would you do me the honour of joining me for lunch at Highgrove tomorrow? 12.30 for 1. Come in your mufti. Charles Rex x' and I smile and tell the footman to tell His Majesty that I'd be delighted to join him, and the footman bows and heads back to Highgrove at a steady trot.

'Now, where were we?' I ask my assistant, and she says somewhere between Jonathan Dimbleby and Jilly Cooper. I say if that's the question, then the answer is always, always dear Jilly. 'Haven't seen Jilly for ages,' I add, reaching for the ashtray. 'See what she's up to. Ask her over for lunch next week. If she says yes put the champers in the fridge right away. Three bottles between the two of us should cover it, but if Annabel turns up make it four. Smoked salmon sandwiches and some of those nice crisps which Charles says are common.' My assistant says, 'Do you mean Walkers?' And I say yes, those are the ones, the roast chicken flavour. 'Can't go wrong with a chicken,' I say absently as she empties the ashtray out of the window and leaves. 'Just shove it in the Aga and hope for the best.'

Still in Wiltshire

I'm at Annabel's for the day, so Charles has written to say that Edward's coming for dinner tomorrow night. 'Nice chap,' I tell Annabel, folding the letter and dismissing the footman who delivered it from Highgrove. 'Bit stodgy, but well meaning. Philip tried to squash him after he came up with *It's a Royal Knockout*. Quite literally, Charles says, under the sofa. He'd sit on it, saying, "Are you still breathing under there?" and if Edward managed to squeak he'd say, "Bit longer, then". Went on for hours. The Corgis were going berserk trying to flush him out and in the end Anne had to stage an intervention. But if you think about it,' I continue, as Annabel pours the drinks, '*It's a Royal Knockout* might be the most interesting thing poor Edward's ever done. Now granted, it was a disaster, but it gave us all a bally good giggle and that's the whole point, isn't it? Can't fault the poor chap for trying.' Annabel says are we quite sure that giving everyone a giggle is the whole point of the royal family? We ponder this and agree that perhaps it isn't and she hands me a G&T. 'Chin chin!' I say, and we settle down for *Homes Under the Hammer.*

15th February
Clarence House, meeting with Clive
to discuss Trooping the Colour

Charles is sitting at his desk with all his pens arranged in order of reliability, and a framed photograph of the topiary at Highgrove. We've already decided that's the one he's going to use for his Christmas address this year, because as I said to Annabel, 'Even bally Harry can't complain if it's a picture of a trimmed bush on his desk. Although I wouldn't put it past him to be peering out from behind it.' Annabel said did I have any idea what I'd just said, about the trimmed bush and Harry, and I said what on earth do you mean? What's the matter with talking about topiary? Anyway, there's a knock at the door and Clive walks in with a folder marked 'Ceremonial 101' and Bluebell in hot pursuit. 'OFF!' I shout and she banks sharply to the right and jumps onto my lap. 'Good girl,' I say and Clive shoots her a dirty look.

'I saw that,' I say. 'I know,' he replies, 'but Bluebell didn't and that's what concerns me. Anyway. You, sir, are going to ride in the procession again, I believe?' Charles says yes that's correct. 'And you, ma'am, will be in a carriage?' And I say yes, although nobody has any idea how bally uncomfortable they are. They make Ginny look like the state Bentley. Clive says, 'Who's Ginny?' Then I'm struck by a brilliant idea.

'I could ride too, alongside my husband,' I say, but Clive says that's out of the question. 'Queen Elizabeth used to do it,' I say.

'Yes,' he says, 'but she rode sidesaddle wearing a skirt. You'd be astride and wearing jodhpurs with a cigarette. Not very regal.' I say well Anne doesn't sit sidesaddle and Clive thinks about it and says no, but she does look terrific in a hat with a red feather sticking up from it, even though she usually has straw in her hair. 'And besides,' he concludes, 'it's different because Anne isn't the Queen. You are. And also,' he adds, 'have you ever tried to tell Anne she's going to do something that she doesn't want to do? Or vice versa?' We all fall silent and consider that chilling prospect, and Clive, with impeccable timing, says, 'Quite. Carriage it is.'

'The problem with carriages,' I tell him, 'is that they're made of wood, so I can't smoke.' Clive says there are possibly other reasons why smoking in carriages isn't a good idea. Then it hits me.

'Actually,' I say, 'if there isn't an illuminated sign

saying "Smoking is not allowed" then technically it IS allowed. So maybe I will,' and I motion to the urn footman to get ready.

'There isn't an illuminated sign saying "Emergency exit" either,' Clive replies mildly, 'but it's still fairly obvious that one should exit via the door.' I pretend not to hear and make a mental note to see if jumping over the side might be viable.

16th February
Buckingham Palace

Clive turns to the page in his Trooping the Colour folder marked 'Difficult siblings (I)'.

'Andrew,' he says, raising his eyebrows and looking at Charles. 'What do we do about him?'

'That specific day?' I ask. 'Or more generally?' Clive says usually both, but today just the former.

'Nothing to do with me,' says Charles firmly, rolling his finger across his pens like the strings on a harp. 'You deal with him.' Clive says he'd be delighted but he struggles for ideas which don't involve The Tower. I consider telling him that even the really damp rooms down by the river have Wi-Fi and are quite comfortable these days, but he's looking misty-eyed. His ideal scenario for Andrew, he says, almost wistfully, would be somewhere remote, cut off by the sea, and only accessible via a badly maintained causeway during certain phases of the moon. 'I hear the more remote

Hebridean islands are wonderful at this time of year,' I say to no one in particular and Clive says yes, but other people live there and that's hardly fair.

'Oh very well then,' says Charles, 'I have an idea. Tell him he can wear his garter robes and raise his flag and watch the Trooping the Colour ceremony in the 3D surround sound cinema room at Windsor Castle. Is that important enough for him? Assuming that he hasn't got one at Royal Lodge?' Clive says he believes not, but his latest intelligence from there was last week and who knows what Fergie might have foraged from a skip since then. 'It'll be almost as good as the real thing,' says Charles, 'a full immersive experience for him, entirely out of sight, away from public view.'

'Immersive and yet sadly without being actually dunked in cold water,' I mutter and Clive says he'll make the necessary arrangements and leaves. Bluebell looks at me hopefully but I tap her muzzle lightly and say 'Off!' and she lies down again.

18th February
Clarence House

Evening in with Annabel. Charles is at White's doing the King thing with William. It seems to be a regular event now, I tell Annabel, which is fine by us because we're starting on *Succession*, now we've finished *Bridgerton*. 'Isn't it terrible that some families have such terrible feuds over money and status,' I say.

141

'Yes,' she says, 'so nothing at all like your own. Although to be fair your family's fights tend to end with a cracked dog bowl.' We chuckle and I upend the Chardonnay into our glasses and call for another. 'How about a few smoked salmon nibbly things to soak it up?' I say to her. 'And maybe a salty snack? Have we got any salted peanuts?' I ask the footman, and he says of course, Duchy Organic or KP?

'Need you ask?' I say. 'KP of course. Whoever heard of organic peanuts?'

'Quite right too,' says Annabel, taking a swig. 'Not on your nelly. Got to be KP. Very fond of a salted peanut. Terribly vulgar and horribly fattening, but frightfully good.'

The footman returns a moment later with a silver punchbowl filled with peanuts and places it carefully on the pouffe and departs. I press play on *Bridgerton* and damn me if that dashed attractive duke isn't doing something really quite unmentionable to his wife on the stairs. Annabel and I goggle at the screen. 'He'll pull a muscle if he isn't careful,' she says, and we roar with laughter and outside the window I hear the footman taking up a precautionary position.

19th February
Clarence House

Annabel thinks the decor needs a refresh so we staged a dawn raid on OKA before it was open. Diana used to do it in Harvey Nicks for the clothes, but Annabel's more of a velvet pouffe sort of girl and she's trying to get me interested in a modular sofa. 'A modular sofa?' I said. 'I'm really not sure Charles will get along with a modular sofa. Sounds frightfully new-fangled and complicated. He's more of a Chippendale man,' but she was adamant.

'What we have to ask ourselves is this,' I told her firmly. 'Is a modular sofa something the early Georgians would have liked? Because that's our market when it comes to my husband.' All she did was roll her eyes.

'Trust me,' she says, 'they're super comf, great for when we're watching *Succession* and so much more *moderne* than bally Chippendale.' In the end I shrugged and, sensing victory, she said, 'Who the baddest bitch?' I said, 'You', and she nodded to the sales assistant who put a big red SOLD sticker on the modular sofa. We bought lots of side tables that look like they came as a job lot from an Indian IKEA, a selection of velvet pouffes ('We love a pouffe,' said Annabel. 'So versatile'), a rattan drinks tray, half a dozen shagreen leather tissue box holders, because nobody wants a Kleenex box on their Georgian dressing table, several pairs of book-ends in the shape of a whippet, a selection of rattan dog beds, a stone pineapple of no obvious usefulness and a lacquered Chinese screen. 'We could make Clive stand behind it when he's saying things we don't want to hear,' I suggest.

Annabel was in her element, issuing lengthy

instructions about artificial orchids and pale blue hydrangeas. Marvellous things, she said, artificial orchids, put them on top of the mahogany tallboy and you'd never know the difference. Gift that keeps on giving. One just has to remind the staff to dust them from time to time. She was about to run amok among the blue Chinese vases when I pointed out we've got the real thing. 'Good point,' she said, turning to the sales assistant. 'Scrap the fake Ming.'

20th February

Up early, another busy day seeing to the revamped decor. We've popped up The Mall in the Bentley to the Queen's Gallery next to Buckingham Palace, where we're meeting the chief curator. 'The clue's in the name,' I told Annabel, 'the Queen's Gallery.'

'Do you have any Canalettos?' I ask the curator and he says yes of course, ma'am, several, and we troop through to where the Canalettos are hanging all in a row.

'Helpful,' I say to the curator. 'Thank you. Now which do you think?' I ask Annabel and the curator looks puzzled. 'Not sure about the red in that one,' she says, pointing to *The Grand Canal with Santa Maria della Salute*. 'Hmm ... that one's too big, that one's too small ... I think this one,' she says finally, peering at a label which says *The Grand Canal looking South-West from the Rialto to Ca' Foscari*. 'And it'd be a pity not to have one of London as well while we're at it,' pointing to *The Thames from Somerset House Terrace towards the City*. 'Good of Canaletto to come here and paint a few of the sights. I don't suppose he painted Clarence House, did he? Or got out to Wiltshire much?' The curator looks apologetic and says he believes not, or at least we don't have any evidence of that in our own collection. Annabel says, 'Never mind, we'll take them both,' and the curator goggles at her and looks from her to me and back again.

'Take them?' he says. 'Where?' I look sharply at him. 'Home, of course,' I say. 'Where else would I take them? Now, where are the horse paintings? Chestnut for preference, goes with everything, about yay big,' and I draw a shape with my hands about four-foot square. 'How about Stubbs? Have you got any nice ones? *Whistlejacket*, can we have a look at that?' The curator seems oddly flustered but tries to recover himself. He says *Whistlejacket* is in the National Gallery and it's very big, much bigger than four-foot square, and he'll need to make a few calls about the Canalettos. Could we possibly come back in the morning? Annabel says absolutely, no problem at all. 'I'm dying for a coffee anyway,' she says. 'Thirsty work this, isn't it?' and we link arms and head out to the Bentley.

21st February

'Are there any more of those about the place?' says Annabel.

'What?' I ask.

'Queen's Galleries,' she says, 'where we can pop in. Scotland, say, or Wales? They might have a horse the right size for above the piano,' and I say I'll ask Clive, but how about lunch out today, round the corner at The Goring? Just a light one, a lobster omelette and a bottle of champers, that sort of thing. 'And let's see if the Brig's in town,' Annabel says, so I scroll through my phone 'til I get to RCB. 'Why's he in your phone as RCB instead of APB?' she asks. I tell her that the security people said we had to give code names for loved ones in case our phones were compromised, so nobody would know who anybody is.

'RCB stands for Rupert Campbell-Black,' I say with a wink. 'Darling Andrew was one of Jilly Cooper's inspirations for the character, you know. Good-looking cad and shagger *extraordinaire*. Awfully cheeky of her, but awfully fun, don't you think? For gawd's sake don't tell Charles,' and I hit 'Call'. Andrew picks up after two rings. 'Your Majesty,' he drawls. 'Do be serious, darling,' I tell him, and he says 'I am being serious, can you doubt it? I'm showing proper deference,' and Annabel snorts at the idea of Andrew deferring to anyone. 'D'you fancy a cheeky lunch at The Goring, with me and Annabel?' I ask, and he says,

'Oh go on then, just a light lobster omelette and a bottle of champers?'

'Yes,' I say happily, 'that's exactly what we had in mind.' I give Annabel the thumbs up and she smiles. Half an hour later, the Bentley pulls up at the door of the hotel and a liveried footman runs down the steps to greet us. 'I'll be repurposing you in about half an hour,' I tell him. 'Second window from the left, round the back, overlooking the garden.'

26th February

I'm in the red saloon flicking a duster over the knick-knacks and watching *Bargain Hunt* with half an eye. 'Keeping it real?' says Annabel, barging in.

'Someone's got to,' I say glumly. 'Charles's idea of keeping it real is wearing a Barbour his son gave him instead of a double-breasted overcoat his father gave him in 1953. I've been cooped up in here since our lunch, all on my own in this bally awful wet weather, without so much as a lobster omelette to sustain me.'

'You're mopey,' she says briskly. 'I can tell. You need a change from socking great hats and fit-and-flare. You need more intellectual stimulation than "Today, I'm thinking emeralds".' It's enough to give a gel a migraine, so I'm springing you from here and we're going out into the real world on an adventure.'

Marvellous, I tell her, a breath of fresh air. Just what the doctor ordered and it's stopped raining at last. Where are we going?

147

'Waitrose,' she says, 'in Belgravia. Lovely branch. It's in a stucco Regency mansion, you'll feel right at home. Not too big, jolly good selection of gin and mixers, deli-style cheese counter and guess what else?'

'What?' I say excitedly. 'Horses?'

'No, it's next door to Mosimann's. We can do a shop at Waitrose then have a jolly lunch there afterwards.'

'Marvellous,' I say again, switching off *Bargain Hunt* and hiding the duster under an embroidered cushion which reads 'No Riff-raff'. 'Mosimann's! My favourite. Are we thinking a little cheese soufflé and a bottle of Picpoul then perhaps a mooch round Cartier?'

'Put these words in the correct order,' says Annabel, 'nail hit head the on,' and she mimes a hammer hitting a nail into the marble-topped chiffonier and the footman winces. 'They're expecting us at Mosimann's at one,' so off we go. 'Look!' I say as we cruise pass Knightsbridge Barracks. 'A horse!'

'D'you think they've got any going spare?' wonders Annabel. 'A nice chestnut that goes with the furniture, perhaps?' I tell her I've got first dibs if they have because I'm the Queen. She rolls her eyes and calls the Brig. 'She's doing the Queen thing,' she says, then passes the phone to me. 'Remember you are mortal,' says Andrew, and in the background I hear a huge crowd cheering. 'You're at the bally races, aren't you?' I tell him crossly. 'You lucky man, did you fancy that filly in the four-forty-five?' Andrew says there's very rarely a filly that he doesn't fancy at four-forty-five, and we chuckle and he says, 'Must dash', and hangs up.

3rd March
A trip to Manchester

Nearly springtime in London, but we're being sent to Manchester to open a mill. 'A mill?' asks Charles. 'That's a little retro, isn't it?' Clive consults his notes and says quite so, sir, you're actually going to open a mall, and he'll have the person who typed this taken out and shot. Charles says steady on, Clive, there's no need to go quite that far and Clive says not to worry, he was only joking, 'That's bally odd,' I said to Charles later when we were cruising up the M6, 'because Clive doesn't do jokes. I must remember to check we've still got a full complement of secretaries when we're back, that one of them hasn't gone missing. One never can tell with Clive.'

'The point is,' says Charles, 'if I wanted jokes, I'd have hired Mike Yarwood, not Clive.'

'Mike Yarwood's dead, darling,' I say, 'and are you sure nobody's made you laugh since 1982?' He says well possibly, but when did Yarwood die? Why did nobody tell him? Nice chap. Terribly good at impressions, he'll write a letter of condolence to his family . . . and how's good old Eric Morecambe these days? I consider saying 'Also dead' but point out some interesting trees instead. 'Look, darling,' I say. 'A conifer.'

Clarence House - that evening

Manchester was fine if you like that sort of thing. Better than Devon, worse than Wiltshire. 'What were you doing up there in the frozen north?' Annabel asked when she called for a catch up. 'Looking delighted,' I said. 'Oh, jolly well done,' she said. 'Not always easy to pull that one off in Manchester. How was the mill?' I explain that it was a mall, not a mill, and behind me Charles says, 'Don't forget to tell her about the conifer, she'll love that.' I turn to look at him fondly and wonder if he has any clue about my darling sister, who wouldn't know a conifer from a concert pianist and isn't interested in either.

4th March

Off to Anmer Hall

We're spending a couple of days at William and Catherine-Kate's little pad in the country.

'I do wish you'd stop calling her that,' says Charles petulantly as we set off.

'But it's funny,' I say, 'don't you think?' and he says

no and I sigh and stare out of the window. Not for the first time I think about the aquamarine tiara and find myself smiling again. We're going so that William and Charles can brainstorm King stuff.

The last time they said they wanted to do this Kate and I asked if they were sure it was a good idea. 'We're fairly sure,' said Kate carefully, 'that the monarchy has survived mostly by turning up and looking delighted, not brainstorming.'

'Well,' I told her, 'credit where it's due, turning up and looking delighted with bally magnificent hair in your case,' and Kate dimples prettily and tells me that my wings are my trademark and Charles reaches out to touch them fondly and I say, 'Don't mess with the Elnett.' He looks wounded and backs off. Anyway, brainstorming seems more of a Clive sort of thing, we told the boys, but Charles says what they mostly talk about is windfarms and biodiversity and Kate and I look at each other and roll our eyes. 'You and I can talk about all the times we've met Mary Berry,' I say, linking my arm through hers as we head for the kitchen. Her eyes light up.

'Wonderful Mary,' she says, 'I sometimes think she's the female David Attenborough, if you know what I mean?' and I say I know exactly what she means: venerable, silver-haired and utterly trustworthy.

'She once showed me the most marvellous compote recipe,' I tell her, 'I must send it to you. It's just the ticket when you've got so many damsons you don't know which way's up,' and Kate says it isn't so much damsons this year as blackcurrants, she's got bally bushels of them in the butler's pantry. Louis keeps squashing them into the soft furnishings and asking when they're going to make Ribena.

'Mary will know what to do with them,' I reassure her, running my finger along the spines of neatly alphabetised cookery books. 'D'you think *Mary Berry's Simple Comforts* or *Mary Berry's Cookery Course* will have the answer?' Kate twinkles and says, 'Ooh, let's live a little, get both of them out,' and puts the kettle on. Just then Louis wanders in waving blackcurrant-coloured hands and leaving blackcurrant-coloured footsteps in his wake. 'Oh god, the carpet,' says Kate, scooping him up and standing him in the kitchen sink before he can do any more damage. 'When are we making Ribena?' he asks and Kate says soon, darling, I promise.

5th March

Anmer Hall

'Anyone fancy a bike ride?' says William. I tell him I haven't ridden a bike since 1979 and I've no intention of riding one now. Why would anyone ride a bike if they could ride a horse? 'Bally baffling,' I say. William says well, the two possibly aren't *directly* comparable or indeed mutually exclusive, but he can see what I mean. Charles brightens at the suggestion of a bike ride and says, 'Have you got any penny farthings?'

William looks at him strangely. 'Penny farthings,' says Charles more loudly, as if William might be hard of hearing. 'Marvellous things. Future of travel. Have I told you about Poundbury?' and William says, 'Righto, Pa, moving on—' and shoos him out the door where the rest of the family is waiting in full Fit Family bike ride gear. 'I'm a Ribena!' says Louis, who's dressed in purple with a purple cycle helmet and purple gloves. Charlotte says, 'Stop showing off, Louis,' and Louis sticks his tongue out. 'Oh god,' says Kate, 'that's purple too,' and off they go.

'Have a wonderful time,' I say, waving them off into a howling Norfolk wind straight off the North Sea. 'Not howling, bracing,' shouts Charles over the gale, and I smile fondly. I tell them I'll be right here next to the Aga with a cup of tea, as many dogs on my lap as care to sit there, and Mary. 'I've found one of her books I've never seen before, *Mary Berry's Complete Cookbook*,' I say to Kate, 'and you wouldn't believe her recipe for lemon poussins with artichoke hearts and a cheeky sprig of rosemary.'

8th March
Clarence House

We're back in London and the papers are full of Harry and Meghan making a spectacle of themselves in New York. Reading the papers would be beneath us, obviously, so William's come round to fill us in. 'Meghan accepted an award for her global advocacy to empower women and girls, but mainly herself,' he tells us. 'Then they complained that they were involved in a "high-speed near-catastrophic car chase around Manhattan for more than two hours", but the Mayor of New York went on TV saying it isn't possible to have a high-speed car chase round Manhattan. But the best bit,' he concludes, 'is when someone from the NYPD said "they arrived safely at their destination and there were no reported collisions, summonses, injuries or arrests".'

We pause to consider this.

'I think,' says Charles with impeccable comic timing, 'that's American for "recollections may vary".'

9th March

The footman is setting up two small gold chairs in front of a vast map of the world on the biggest table we've got. The man from the Foreign Office is coming round to give us a general briefing about where we are.

'I could have told them that,' I tell Charles. 'We're here,' waving towards the North Sea just north of France. 'But joking apart, does he mean us,' I ask, 'or them,' pointing in the direction of the rest of the country, 'or the whole world?' Charles says it's a bit of all three, along with where we are as a family, in the life of the nation. He stands up and looks like he might be about to orate about the role of a constitutional monarchy, but just then Bluebell girds her loins and jumps off the pouffe, heading with intent towards an approaching Clive. The moment passes and he sits down again.

'We're going to visit Samoa and Australia and I think India too, later in the year,' he says, 'and they want us to be up to speed on what we can and can't say.'

'So, India,' says the man from the FO standing in front of us and pointing to India on the map with a riding crop. He asked for a laser pointer but I explained that we don't have many of those lying around. To be fair, he took the proffered crop in his stride. 'Things not to mention,' he continues. 'The Koh-i-Noor, Pakistan, Kashmir, moon landings, nuclear programmes, or the Raj. If we can get in and out without them realising you're English, even better. And definitely don't mention our international aid budget in the same sentence as their moon landings and nuclear programmes. Leave that one to the PM.'

'I could write them a letter about it,' says Charles. 'I expect they'd like some advice on the risks of overfishing in the Bay of Bengal as well.' The man from the FO says we'd be extremely grateful if you didn't write to them, sir, and perhaps we could reconvene tomorrow?

10th March

'Next up: the Middle East,' says the man from the FO. 'We're broadly in favour of the Middle East except when we're not. Clear?' Charles nods and I start to mutter about women's rights and ghastly misogynistic regimes who stone adulterers. The man from the FO blanches and says to Clive, 'Is Her Majesty serious?' and Clive glares at me and says no, Her Majesty has something caught in her throat.

'Yes,' I harrumph, 'my opinions.'

'She'll be quite alright momentarily,' he reassures the man from the FO, who looks uneasy but carries on.

'China. Broadly against, except when we're not,' he says and I put my hand up and he says, 'Yes, the lady at the front there wearing the crown?' I ask, 'Could you clarify what we're against and what we're not and where?' And the man says, 'Excellent question,' says the man, 'I'd be happy to. We're against the murderous suppression of dissent, but we try not to say that out loud in case it upsets people keen on the murderous suppression of dissent. Specifically, we try not to upset those people who have oil, strategic locations, or things we'd like ourselves. For example, precious metals useful in engineering or small islands far from here that are suitable for the Navy to use as a base.'

'Isn't that pretty much everywhere?' I ask and he says yes and changes the subject.

'We're also in favour of them doing what we'd like when it comes to climate change and giving us a favourable post-Brexit trade deal, because even though a trade deal with China is a terrifically exciting and imminent prospect it is also,' and he checks his notes, '5,000 miles away, populated by people who largely don't speak English or want what we sell, and will in no way make up for leaving the gigantic market on our doorstep populated by people who do.'

'Do they all talk like you in the Foreign Office?' I ask and he says yes, as a matter of fact they do.

'Righto,' I say, 'what about beef in black bean sauce? You haven't mentioned that, but Charles and I are very much in favour, aren't we darling? We're quite partial to a Singapore noodle as well. Is that allowed in the same meal, or will it cause a diplomatic incident?' The man from the FO looks at me and then looks at Clive, who shrugs.

That afternoon

We broke for lunch, or at least they did. Charles doesn't approve of lunch which is why Annabel and I have to spend so much of our time locating it off-site at Bentley's. Clive disappears below stairs with the man from the FO, who's looking rather pale. Clive is telling him don't worry, nobody's going to mention ghastly old waxworks any more, we've put all that behind us now, and the man from the FO says he wished he could share Clive's confidence. 'By the way,' I hear him say conversationally as Clive opens the green baize door, 'has anyone removed Andrew's passport yet? Just as a precaution, you know—' Clive murmurs soothing nothings and I smile and the door closes behind them.

That afternoon, I consult my briefing notes and discover that we're very much in favour of Ireland, Scotland and Wales, the Falkland Islands, the British Virgin Islands, St Helena, Anguilla and the Cayman Islands. 'I'm sensing a pattern here,' I say. 'They're all places we own.' The FO man says quite so, it makes life so much easier. Charles mutters, 'For whom?', but the FO man is already onto the United States ('Hard yes'), South America ('tendency to unreliability'), Canada ('chilly with alarming numbers of bears, although the west coast is surprisingly temperate'), Malaysia ('ideal for refuelling en route to Australia') and Australia ('problematic wildlife'). I say sharply to Clive did they get the memo about Australia, i.e. that I'm not going, and Clive says yes, ma'am, but some other member of the royal family might go and our official position on it needs to amount to more than 'Too far'.

'And problematic wildlife achieves that?' I ask, raising my eyebrows, and the man from the FO says Australia's still a work in progress. 'Our view on it,' he adds, 'not the country.'

20th March
Buckingham Palace

Dreadful place, Buck House, never go usually, but Clive was most insistent.

'Welcome to the AGM of the RBP,' says Clive, who's wearing a hi-vis vest and a hard hat. 'Getting into character?' I ask and he glares at me and bangs a gavel to call the meeting to order. 'Gavel,' I say, 'interesting choice,' and Clive says it seemed like a good idea. I tell him a riding crop might be better suited to the job because it usually is. 'And,' I finish, 'must we talk in acronyms as if we're Wiltshire County Council?'

'Is anybody listening to me around here?' says Charles, who's irritable because he fell off his perch this morning when he was doing his bat thing, and jarred his shoulder. The room falls silent while we wait for someone else to say, 'Of course we are, Your Majesty,' but nobody does, so I say, 'Of course we are.' Charles says, 'What does AGM RBP mean? What are we talking about? What are we doing here when I've got a far nicer home up the road?' He starts to slump dejectedly in his seat, when what we actually need at this point is more of the King thing. I pat his arm reassuringly and look to Clive for enlightenment because I haven't a bally clue why we're here either. I just do as I'm told.

'It's the Annual General Meeting of the Redecorating Buckingham Palace committee,' says Clive.

'Out of interest,' says Charles, 'how many AGMs have there been?' Clive consults his notes.

'Twenty-three,' he says, 'not counting leap years, when we had two just in case.' Charles puts his head in his hands and I make for the window but they're all glued shut for replacement. The footman is standing outside looking up at me forlornly. He's trying to sound the alarm, look insouciant, and hold an urn all at the same time.

Official Minutes of the AGM of the RBP

Sir Clive Alderton explained that the building is in a poor state of repair and requires work. The Comptroller of the Household concurred, while pointing out that sources of funding are regrettably opaque and also inadvisable in a strategic manner possibly related to political considerations. The committee questioned him closely on this statement. The meeting broke up with a renewed determination to pursue this worthwhile project of national and international historical importance, while also keeping costs down to a historic low of zero. The King was moved to give his most gracious consent. The Queen concurred.

Unofficial Minutes of the AGM of the RBP

Sir Clive Alderton in the chair. The comptroller said: 'The building is falling down round our ears. Nobody has done anything to it since 1872, nobody has wanted to do anything to it since 1962, nobody will pay anything for it until 2122. It will fall down many years before that, in approximately 2042. The

King said he hadn't a bally clue what the Comptroller is on about, and blamed Clive, who blamed the Cabinet Secretary, who was roundly berated by all assembled for being present at all. The Cabinet Secretary said he needed to make sure that the budget for repairs came in at approximately £0 at which point Bluebell and Beth began to bark. The meeting broke up in disarray with wild and unsubstantiated rumours that the King muttered "Rats in a bally sack" and fled, while the Queen said, "It's a bally dump anyway, nobody wants anything to do with it, and if you think I'm moving here from over the road you've another think coming. Not when Annabel's just bought a job lot of new pouffes and a modular sofa."'

That evening

'I've been thinking,' I say to Charles, 'if the balcony at Buckingham Palace is the most important thing, symbolically, Annabel says there's no reason at all we can't just chisel it off, stick it on Clarence House and have done with it. It's not as if anyone'll know the difference,' I add. 'We hardly ever use it and when we do everyone's looking at Louis or the Red Arrows.'

'And me,' says Andrew who's popped in, looking hopeful. 'I can put on a hell of a show in my garter robes and plumed hat, and Buck House has a truly wonderful flagpole and a gigantic flag. Really something to aspire to,' he says. Charles glares at him.

'Relocating the balcony isn't a problem,' says the comms guy. 'We'll just have to crop the picture in close, and as long as it's hi-res no one will know if the postcode's SW1 or Slough.'

'Did somebody say Slough?' says Charles. 'I've got big plans for Slough. Penny farthings. Picket fences. Gracious squares named after my dear Grandmama. Corinthian columns. You wait.'

I think I hear Clive mutter something about come, friendly bombs, but I'm tired so I could be mistaken.

2nd April

Charles needs a new head gardener for Highgrove and he's agonising over how to word the advert. Should it mention the topiary specifically? he asks. The stumpery? The importance of maintaining the sanctity of the Coronation Canopy? Or should it approach the subject more generally, in terms of the ethos of Highgrove, his personal commitment to organic gardening and keen interest in bees? I stifle a yawn. I've got my feet up on one of his bally uncomfortable wooden sofas, because I eventually lost the argument over Annabel's modular updates. I look at him over the top of my reading glasses.

'First,' I say to him, 'this sofa is bally uncomfortable. Next time Annabel says we need something in a nubbly oatmeal linen from OKA that won't clash with the curtains, then we are getting something in a nubbly oatmeal linen from OKA that won't clash with the curtains. And,' I say, picking up the phone and calling her, 'as luck would have it, she is literally just about to

tell you herself.' I hand him the phone and he sighs
and I hear Annabel talking to him. 'And in the mean-
time,' I say to Charles when she's finished, 'can't we
get some decent cushions? You can get lovely ones on
Etsy with wonderful mottos embroidered on them.
I've just got a new one with "Jack Russells Rock" on
it, and Annabel's got one with "Champers, anyone?"
It's navy, goes with everything, even the horses as long
as they're not piebald.' He looks at me as if I'm mad.

'Why do cushions need to have things written on
them?' he says. 'And can we get back to my advertise-
ment for a gardener?'

'Yes,' says Anne, who's popped in to borrow my
Tattersalls catalogue. 'How about this: "Head
gardener needed, green fingers preferred". Honestly,
Charles, why do you have to make everything so bally
difficult? You're worse than Andrew.'

'To be fair, at least Charles doesn't make things difficult on national television,' I say. 'And he hardly ever
goes out in public wearing a velvet cape and a hat with
a feather.' Anne says yes, that's true, but hiring someone who knows a tulip from a teacup really isn't that
difficult, and Charles winces and says there's far too
many bally women in this room. He stomps out to
look for Clive and I can hear him saying, 'Get Alan
Titchmarsh on the phone, I need to talk to him about
stumperies. And find out if he'd like a new job.'

9th April
Highgrove

Charles has tasked me with casting my eye over the workshop courses at Highgrove. Nice little money-spinner for the foundation, according to Clive. Those Christmas wreath workshops and Tuesday morning mulled wine seminars keep the coffers nicely topped up, he told his deputy Chris, when he thought I wasn't listening.

'Check that the classes reflect our values,' Charles said, opening his Red Box to start work and waving vaguely towards the Coronation Canopy or possibly Gloucestershire more generally.

'Do you mean the values of the Coronation Canopy or Gloucestershire more generally?' I ask and he says hard to tell, probably both, you decide. I go over to Annabel's and recruit her to help. 'Bally hell,' she says, 'I don't even know if my values align with the dogs, let alone Charles, but let's have a crack,' and we settle down at the kitchen table with a packet of chocolate Hobnobs.

'Righto,' I say, drinking tea from a chipped *EastEnders* mug with Den and Angie on it. 'Where on earth did you get this?' I ask. 'Where's the Emma Bridgewater? She does a lovely pattern with dogs, you know.' Annabel looks blankly at Den and Angie and shrugs. 'Fergie? Anyway. "Workshop number one: loose covers for beginners". What do we think? Aligned with Charles's values or just Gloucestershire more generally?'

167

'Gloucestershire more generally,' I say. 'Charles wouldn't know a loose cover from a loose box.'

'Good lord, it lasts for two days!' says Annabel incredulously, going through the blurb about the loose covers. '"This course will take you through the process of making a loose cover for an armchair". Er, hello?' she says, miming making a phone call. 'Is that OKA? Please could I BUY a bally armchair?' and we laugh and I spill my tea on the floor and the dogs lick it up.

'"Workshop number two",' she continues. '"Creating a gathered lampshade: an introduction. This course will include the opportunity to make your own gathered lampshade" – no, really? I would never have guessed – "and learn more about how to bind a lampshade frame and measure a lampshade". Your thoughts on the gathered lampshade workshop, beloved sister?'

'Perturbed,' I say, dunking a Hobnob. 'Firstly, that people might know what a gathered lampshade is. Secondly, learn how to measure a lampshade? Even Fergie could manage that, from the bottom of a skip. Surely you just need a tape measure?' Annabel shrugs and says the OKA catalogue tells you that sort of thing. 'And thirdly,' I say, 'I'm perturbed as to why anyone might care enough about lampshades to pay £80 to learn how to make one when they could be doing something useful, like walking the dogs. So I vote we scrap that one. Not so much aligned with our values as no one's, and borderline subversive in its pointlessness.'

'Too bally right,' says Annabel, putting a red line through it. 'If they need a lampshade, what do they think Peter Jones is for? Speaking of which, I'm meeting darling Fiona for a coffee there next Thursday and a mooch round the bras. Excellent selection for the more mature lady,' and she squishes her bosoms like Les Dawson used to do and I laugh. 'Do come,' she says. I pull my diary out of my bag on the floor and groan. 'I'm in Oswestry,' I say. 'Oswestry?' she says. 'What on earth are you doing in Oswestry?'

'Looking delighted,' I say and she pats my arm sympathetically and we go back to the courses.

'"Number 3," she reads, "introduction to chair caning . . ."'

11th April
Windsor Castle

William convened a meeting to discuss the Royal Warrant Holders and we're all there. Charles, Anne, Andrew, Edward, Sophie, Clive and Kate with Louis on her lap because she can't get child care. Charles asks why she couldn't just leave him with the footman? but Kate says they don't have any footmen. Charles gapes. 'How utterly extraordinary my dear,' he says, 'however do you manage your toothpaste?' Kate smiles kindly at him and says, 'Easy when you know how,' and Louis makes a lunge for a passing dog.

William's in the chair. Charles thinks the Royal

Warrants are a marvellous way to celebrate the nation's rich heritage and cultural assets. 'They are,' he says, standing up and hooking his thumb in his pocket in preparation for the King thing, 'a marvellous way to celebr—' William says yes, Pa, we know, no need to give it the full Cicero, and Charles sits down again. The gist of William's thinking is that the whole system should be swept away in favour of sustainable plastic development and more seaweed farms. Or something. I'm not entirely sure what, but I am entirely sure that I don't care. 'I mean,' William once remarked to Charles, 'does anyone really notice who makes our tea towels?' to which Charles replied, 'What's a tea towel?' Today, William's in bullish form. 'The system of Royal Warrants is,' he says, concluding his opening remarks, 'an archaic form of semi-feudal nonsense that should be swept away.'

'Like the Duchy of Cornwall?' says Anne brightly, without looking up from the Tattersalls catalogue. 'The estate that funds you?'

'No,' says William, 'nothing like the Duchy of Cornwall.' Anne holds her hands up in mock defeat and says, 'Whatever you say, sire,' and goes back to the yearlings. William gives her a filthy look. He's handed us all a list of the eight hundred current Warrant Holders and it occurs to me for the first time that he might actually be intending to go through them, one by one. 'I'm due at Mosimann's at one for lunch with Fiona and it's already eleven-thirty,' I whisper in a panic to Charles. He says he can't abide lunch himself, terrible idea, which doesn't help me one bit. I look over to the window in desperation, and the footman standing there gives me a discreet thumbs up to say the troops are in position.

'So,' says William, 'let's begin at the beginning,' and I suppress a groan and back slowly towards the window without making eye contact with anyone.

Ten minutes later

They're still on the As.

'A. C. Bacon Engineering Ltd,' says William, 'A. C. Beck and Son (Contracts) Ltd, A. C. Cooper (Colour) Limited, A. J. Freezer Water Services. Who are they, what do they do and why should we care? Anyone?' He looks around the table and we all look blank. 'Well someone must know why they've got a Royal Warrant?' But nobody does, so he marks them with a highlighter pen and carries on.

'A. Nash.'

'Any relation to the chap who built Regents Park?' asks Charles cheerfully, but no one hears him except me. I pat his arm and say I expect he is, darling, we must have him over for tea and see what he thinks about Poundbury, and Charles looks gratified.

'Carluccio's?' says William, looking perplexed. 'Why on earth does Carluccio's have a Royal Warrant?'

'Tortellini,' says Kate. Everyone looks at her and Charles says, 'Bless you.'

'The tortellini are excellent,' she says. 'The children love them and Mummy takes them to the branch in

Windsor for tea as a special treat after school if we can't do pick-up.' William says well in that case they clearly need at least one Royal Warrant, richly deserved, and moves on.

'Champagne Bollinger, Krug, Lanson, Moet, Veuve Clicquot,' he reads, and I put my hand up. 'Me! I couldn't choose just one so we put them all on. You'll find Pol Roger further down when you get to Ps at about half past six this evening.' William eyes me speculatively to see if I'm joking and starts to continue, but I sense my chance.

'If we can have French Champagne houses could we also have French fashion houses on there?' I say. 'Like Dior and Chanel and Yves Saint Laurent? I've always rather fancied a Le Smoking—'

'Why?' says Anne. 'Because of the smoking?'

'By the way before you ask,' I say to William, ignoring her, 'yes, Clarins UK is me too. Marvellous moisturiser for the more mature lady.' William looks horrified, Anne turns the pages noisily until she gets to stallions and Andrew sneezes. Everyone glares at him and tells him to be quiet.

'Claydon Horse Exercisers?' says William.

'Me!' says Anne, and William asks if horse exercisers are strictly necessary. He thought they were called 'riders', not Claydon, and how much money does she spend on not riding her own horses? Anne says probably about half what William spends on helicopter fuel. William eyes her speculatively, too.

'Corgi Hosiery Ltd,' he continues, and we all hoot

with laughter. Do Corgis need hosiery? I ask Clive and he says Andrew's the one with the Corgis these days. Andrew says he'll check with Fergie. 'Couldn't she source the hosiery from a skip?' I mutter to Clive. William points at Andrew with his highlighter pen and says he wants a detailed breakdown of exactly how much is spent on Corgi hosiery in any given year and Andrew says that's completely impossible. 'Why?' says William. 'Because I have no idea,' says Andrew, 'and I can hardly ask the Corgis, can I?' Clive starts explaining that it's a company which makes tights, it just happens to be called Corgi, but nobody hears him because Andrew's ploughing on, digging his own grave. 'Most importantly of all,' he's saying, 'I'm not going to find out because it's none of your business.' A hush falls on the room as he looks around delightedly, expecting applause for his augmented intellect and demolition of William's argument. 'And,' he says, ploughing on, 'AND never forget that those Corgis are our last link to my beloved Mama, who specifically entrusted them to Fergie and myself—'

'I rather thought you brought them and they just reverted back to you when she died,' mutters Anne. Andrew glares at her and William says ENOUGH of the Corgi hosiery and puts a neat line through it on his list and smiles at Andrew, who scowls and we break for lunch.

2 p.m.

'Croford Coachbuilders,' he says. Charles puts his hand up.

'Realistically, Pa, how many coaches are we going to need to build in the coming months and years?' asks William. Charles says well, that's a very good question and he's glad William asked it, because we've got a state visit to Australia coming up. It might be a fitting tribute to commission a coach, he says, made out of eucalyptus wood with paintings of koalas and kangaroos on the doors.

'So to recap,' says Anne, who's becoming increasingly cheerful as the meeting progresses, 'you're going to spend a fortune on an eighteenth-century mode of transport covered in patronising clichés for a visit to a country that doesn't care?' Charles starts to protest that travelling by coach is an exceptionally climate-friendly mode of transport. 'Zero emissions apart from the horses and you can use that on the roses,' he says, and the whole room stares at him.

William tells Clive to ensure that under no circumstances is there to be any contact whatsoever between Clarence House and Croford Coachbuilders now or at any point in the future. If anyone starts asking discreet questions about sourcing eucalyptus wood he is to be informed immediately.

'What if I'm at Birkhall not Clarence House?' says Charles. 'Can I make contact from there? Could Croford come to meet me in Scotland?' William says we're going to take a fifteen-minute break for him to bang his head repeatedly against the wall, and I make a dash for the window. The footman grins up and throws me a lit B&H.

'I took the precaution of moving your lunch to tomorrow, ma'am,' he says. 'I hope that was in order,' I give him the thumbs up.

15 minutes later

'Right. Flying Colours Flagmakers Ltd,' says William. We all turn round and look at Andrew who says, 'Why is everyone looking at me? You all have flags too.'

'Not on poles,' says William, 'on top of our houses.'

'Unless we're the King,' says Charles, 'and you're not.'

Andrew says yes, well, so what if it was him who gave the flagmakers the Royal Warrant? And what if they are located conveniently next to an outstanding golf course? And as it happens he's going there on an official visit a week on Tuesday and it's very likely they'll give him a new flag. 'They're thinking a big image of York Minster,' he says, 'obviously in honour of my title. All very tasteful,' and we all speak at once.

'How are you getting there?' says William.

'How much will it cost?' says Clive. Charles stands up and hooks his thumb in his pocket.

'NO!' he thunders. 'To everything. There will be no trip, no golf and no new flag.' Clive says would now be a good time to talk about downsizing Andrew to somewhere without Royal in the name or flags on the roof? Andrew says it isn't his fault he can't afford the upkeep of a thirty-room mansion, nobody gives him any money any more. He looks pointedly at William, which is a mistake. 'Oh dear,' William says. 'Has someone clamped down on foreign billionaires overpaying you for houses? Are oligarchs not as rich or friendly as they used to be?' Andrew says no, actually, so what would they have him do instead?

'Move,' says Charles.

'Leave,' says Clive.

'The nightshift at Sainsbury's,' says William.

Final session

'Can I just say,' I say, putting my hand up at the beginning, 'that it is precisely seventy-five minutes until six o'clock? Good to have a liquid deadline, and I'm parched.'

'Before you ask,' says Anne, raising her hand, 'Mobile Farrier Services, M. R. J. Farriers and the National Foaling Bank are all me. And no,' she adds, clocking William's expression, 'I do not care to explain why I need more than one farrier. Do you need more than one helicopter?' William starts to say no, but Anne isn't listening. 'I rest my case,' she says.

'Parker Pen company,' says William, accepting defeat, 'no prizes for guessing that one. But Serena Richards T/A Slightly Potty? Extraordinary name for a company.'

'Me,' I say. 'Bally lovely silk flowers in pots.'
Everyone stares at me as if requiring an explana-
tion. 'Well I can't get them all from bally OKA,
can I?'

'Tanqueray gin, the Pimm's Company—'

'Me again!' I say brightly. 'Sixty-five minutes and
counting.'

'VW Group UK.'

'Me!' says Anne and I glare at her. 'I paid up front
for Ginny!' I tell her resentfully and Anne shrugs and
says if Peter can get free milk from the Chinese why
can't she get free cars from the Germans? William
says he has literally no idea what we're talking about,
so Clive shows him the video on YouTube of Peter
flogging milk to the Chinese. He groans.

'Does Peter really need to go to China to get milk?'
Charles asks Anne. 'Couldn't he find it closer to home?
In a cow?'

'Finally: Weetabix Ltd,' says William. 'Could someone, anyone, please explain to me why Weetabix need
a royal warrant?'

'Louis,' says Kate. 'Look on the bright side, darling,
it could be worse. At least it isn't Coco Pops.'

15th April

Meeting with a producer from CBBC, an earnest
American, oddly, who wants me to read the bedtime
story. 'Americans at the BBC!' I say cheerfully. 'Does
anyone ever tell you the barbarians are at the gate?'

She looks startled and says no, ma'am, they don't. Reading the bedtime story is an institution, she tells me, lots of people have done it including Kate, so all above board, no nasty surprises or sudden Emily Maitlises when the cameras are rolling. 'Have any other Queens done it?' I ask and she says yes, but not the royal kind. 'What book are you thinking of reading?' I tell her Beatrix Potter's *The Tale of the Flopsy Bunnies* and she looks blank.

'Beatrix Potter's a British national treasure,' I say. 'Wonderful stuff.'

'Sounds great,' she says. 'What's the plot?'

'Small rabbits kidnapped by scary old man narrowly avoid being eaten.'

'Got it,' she says, putting a line through *The Tale of the Flopsy Bunnies*. 'Any other ideas?'

'*The Tale of Peter Rabbit*,' I say. 'Small rabbit terrorised by scary old man narrowly avoids being put in a pie. Unlike his father, who was.'

She looks at me.

'I'm sensing a theme here.'

'Not at all,' I say, 'very versatile, Beatrix Potter. If you're after short stories of small animals meeting untimely deaths, there's something for everyone. But I understand, rabbits aren't your thing. How about *The Tale of Samuel Whiskers*?'

'Whiskers!' she says, brightening. 'Cute cat?'

'Yes and no,' I say. 'Thieving murderous rat kidnaps kitten and tries to eat him for dinner.'

She looks horrified.

'*Jemima Puddleduck*?' I try. 'Thick duck groomed by devious fox to lay her eggs in his house.'

'And?' she says. 'The fox gets it, the ducklings survive and everyone lives happily ever after on the village pond?'

'Yes and no,' I say, 'but mostly no.'

'I have a better idea,' she says. 'How about *The Bench* by your daughter-in-law?'

'Kate's written a book?' I say.

'No,' she says brightly, 'the other daughter-in-law, Meghan.'

'Shush . . .' I say, 'don't talk so loud. What's it about?'

'A bench,' she says. 'Nothing happens. Nobody dies. You'll love it.'

18th April
Ray Mill House

I'm sitting in the dog bed next to the Aga reading bedtime stories to Bluebell and Beth. 'Practising on the dogs,' I tell Kate. I've called her for style advice ahead of my primetime CBBC debut. 'Will the fit-and-flare do the job?' I ask. 'Low-key jewels so the glare doesn't wake up the little blighters, easy on the Elnett, that sort of thing?' Kate says no, think more Wiltshire mufti but luxe it up a bit. 'Luxe it up?' I say. 'What on earth does "luxe it up" mean?' There's silence for a moment while Kate thinks about the question. 'It means clean,' she says in the end. 'Less dog hair. Fewer poo bags. Also, that chicken drumstick poking out of your pocket last time I saw you?'

'Bally useful things, spare chicken legs,' I say, 'won't hear a word said against them. You never know when a spare chicken leg in your pocket might come in useful.' In my lap, Bluebell twitches in her sleep and woofs softly.

'Perhaps,' says Kate, 'but I know when a chicken leg definitely won't be useful, and that's on national television while you're reading a bedtime story. What are you going to read, anyway?' I tell her that's a work in progress but we're thinking one of the Mr Men books.

'Nobody dies,' I tell her. 'They seem quite keen on that. American, you know.'

20th April
Birkhall

We've come to Scotland for Charles to spend time at Birkhall and me to get cold. 'I need to keep moving,' I tell Charles. 'It's bally freezing up here, did I mention that?' And he says yes possibly I have mentioned that, every day in fact, since we got married. To stave off the cold we go to Dumfries House, to meet the new gardener and unofficially check how many times we can see the word 'heritage' and 'rare breed' while standing in one spot.

'I make it 427,' says Charles. 'Do we think that's too many or about right?' Clive's scrolling through the online guidebook and says well perhaps we could afford to lose a few without diminishing the overall effect. 'There's even stuff in here about the animals and rare breeds they have on the estate,' he says. 'Fascinating, and goodness me, "Crollwitzer turkeys are a personal favourite of His Majesty",' he reads. 'Who knew?'

'Me,' says Charles.

Later

Charles and I are proof-reading blurb for the Dumfries House website, newly rewritten to his detailed specifications. 'Have we still got the Crollwitzer turkeys in there?' he asks and I say absolutely, darling, Clive wouldn't have it any other way. 'In fact,' I lie fluently, 'he said that guidebooks in twenty-first-century England are hopeless without a colourful reference to a Crollwitzer turkey.'

'Dumfries House is in Scotland, not England,' says Charles. I say yes, that's probably what Clive meant, but it's all the same really. Charles looks alarmed and says no, Scotland and England aren't the same at all, and could I not say things like that out loud, in public?

'Why does everyone keep saying that to me?' I complain. Charles says he can't imagine but it's possibly not unconnected to me saying things that I shouldn't say, out loud, and in public. It's after dinner, just the two of us, 'Super casual, no crowns,' I joke to the butler, who looks appalled. We're sitting side-by-side at matching Chippendale writing desks lit by four-branched candlesticks. 'You'd better move those,' I tell the footman, waving at my hair, which hasn't moved an inch since breakfast. 'Elnett. I'll go up in flames.'

We've told most of the staff to have the night off so we can be more private. 'Skeleton staff only,' said Charles. He takes the seat offered by the footman, chooses a pen from a selection offered by another footman and a glass of whisky from a silver salver held by another. 'I love it when we have informal evenings like this,' he sighs, 'just you and me,' as a fourth footman banks the fire, a fifth corrals the dogs, a sixth asks if he has any specific requests regarding his toothpaste at bedtime and the underbutler takes up position behind his chair. Charles begins to read the blurb out loud.

'"The five-acre walled garden is one of the biggest in Scotland and features a unique twelve-metre drop from north to south." Well I think that's perfect, darling, don't you?' he says, looking up. 'Fascinating and informative.'

'Absolutely,' I say, 'if we're sure that talking about a twelve-metre drop is the way to pull the punters in?'

'Oh?' says Charles.

'All I'm saying,' I say carefully, 'is it means "slope". We're saying "Come to Dumfries House and admire a magnificent slope".' Charles looks deflated and says oh well when I put it like that and turns to the bit about the Chinese bridge. I resolve to tell Clive that my husband is to be kept well away from this sort of thing in future or he'll bore the punters to death before they've even left home. Charles has started reading aloud about the Chinese bridge.

'"The story of its construction, especially the numerous contractors and tonnes of steel required to create it, surely adds to its magic",' he reads, nodding approvingly and I realise Marlboro Lights won't touch the sides tonight. '"The pewter corridor forms a right angle",' he continues, turning the page, '"the original polychrome survived under the grey—"' On the floor, as far away as possible from the fire, Bear starts to snore gently, with a sleepy Jack Russell on his back and another across his paws. I look at them sympathetically and wish, not for the first time, that I were a dog.

'"The vegetable garden is one of the finest in eastern Ayrshire, with an excellent selection of rare breed celeriac",' Charles reads. I resist the urge to say, 'No detail too small' and allow myself to nod off.

21st April
Clarence House

Back in London and Clive has arrived to discuss the property situation with us. I notice that he's brought along a short man in a suit.

'Who are you?' I ask.

'Still the prime minister,' he says and I peer at him over my reading glasses.

'Have we met?' and he bows.

'Nope,' I say, 'ringing no bells but not your fault, don't take it personally. If you were a horse I'd recognise you at twenty paces. But you're not.'

'No,' he says, looking slightly demoralised, 'I'm the prime minister.'

'Why is this meeting called a property situation?' interrupts Charles. 'Doesn't one simply have property? Why is having property a situation?'

'Because there's rather a lot of it,' says the short man who says he's the prime minister, but one can never be sure. 'We've counted it up and you own 7 palaces, 10 castles, 12 houses, 14 ancient ruins and 56 cottages.'

'Fourteen ancient ruins?' I say. 'Does that include us?' I wink at Charles who frowns and the prime minister coughs and says this is no laughing matter, ma'am.

Clive says it might be helpful to categorise the various properties, recategorise the ones that are problematic, and limit the amount of time we stay anywhere with 'palace' or 'castle' in the name. 'Particularly,' he adds, 'if we've just briefed the press that we're streamlining the royal finances and bankrupting Andrew in the national interest. So. Highgrove?'

'House,' says Charles.

'Clarence?'

'House,' says Charles.

'Ray Mill?'

'Hovel,' says Charles.

'Beloved family home,' I correct him.

'Beloved family hovel,' Charles tells Clive, and I decide that now would be an excellent time for an appointment with an urn.

'If you'll excuse me,' I say politely to the short man, 'I have an urgent appointment with an urn,' and he looks for guidance at Clive, who is studiously not looking at him.

'Kensington?' asks Clive, ignoring us both.

'Palace,' says Charles, and Clive puts a neat line through it and adds that he's going to recategorise Birkhall as a modified bungalow.

'Finally, Llwynywermod?' he says, not without difficulty.

'Cottage,' says Charles, 'barely more than five bedrooms, poky little place, and besides, we've given it up.'

'He isn't the Prince of Wales any more so there's no need to pretend we're interested in Wales, let alone go there,' I tell him. 'Over to William and Kate on that one. *Bara brith Cymru*, as they say.' Clive says he thinks *bara brith* is the name of a type of bread and he's fairly sure I mean *Hwyl fawr*, but whatever I mean I shouldn't be saying it out loud, in public, in front of the prime minister. I tell him however you say it, we're not going there again and take a long drag of my ciggie. Just then my phone rings on the pouffe and I flick the butt into the urn. It's the Brig, giving me an update from the Hinge frontline.

'The corker from Bayswater,' I whisper. 'How did it go?'

'Glass of champagne at Duke's then Bentley's,' he says. 'Putty in my hands.'

'Did you have her at *Bore da*?' I tease and he says why are you speaking Welsh, she's from west London. I tell him it's a long story.

'Anyway, it turns out all the nice gels love a briga-dier,' he says and we start to laugh and Clive and Charles and the short man look curiously at me. 'Must dash,' I tell him. '*Hwyl fawr*,' and hang up.

22nd April

'What's the jewel situation at Trooping the Colour?' I ask my stylist, who's a librarian. Books are far more interesting than clothes, so why would I hire someone to talk about clothes? 'Do the jewels tend to be big? Or little?' I ask, and she rifles through the back catalogue of *Hello!* magazines we keep for research purposes and says, 'They seem to be discreet.' I sag with disappointment. 'Unreasonable to suppose that every day can be a bling day, but still. There's a hell of a lot of bling for me to get through and I'm not getting any younger.' She nods sympathetically and says maybe tomorrow, ma'am. I brighten and say yes, actually, I'm meeting Annabel for a coffee at Peter Jones tomorrow and if ever a department store was bling-tolerant, it's Peter Jones. Although tiaras on a Tuesday might be pushing it. 'That shop's by appoint-ment to bally all of us,' I say, 'and they have an excel-lent selection of bras for the more mature figure.' The librarian looks horrified and says yes ma'am, and leaves.

25th April
Weekend at Birkhall

I'm checking my William Hill account on the iPad when Charles looks over my shoulder and reads out the warning. '"Gamble Responsibly". I suppose they mean don't bet the house. Or in our case the palace. Or,' he pauses for comedic effect, 'the Crown Jewels!' and he chortles to himself and wanders over to the bookshelves. It's an important day, because the Keeper of the Privy Purse is coming to talk to us about how we spend the Sovereign Grant and I'm under strict orders not to mention the urn footman.

'Excellent title,' I tell him, when he's shown in. 'Do you have a name, too?' and I look expectantly at Clive who says Your Majesties, may I introduce Sir Michael? who bows and begins.

'6th September 2022 train Kemble–Darlington.'

'Ah, yes,' I say, 'I remember it well.' Sir Michael says really ma'am? That's very impressive and I say of course not, but I expect we left Kemble looking delighted, and arrived in Darlington looking positively thrilled. Sir Michael bows and says the trip cost £27,645 and I gasp.

'Even with the Senior Railcards?' I say, and Sir Michael says he doesn't think Senior Railcards are valid on the Royal Train so I tell him sharply that discounts are always available if you are flexible on dates and book early enough. Sir Michael looks at Clive for support, but Clive's staring fixedly at the cornice.

'9th September private charter from residence to residence in support of London Bridge/Spring Tide, £25,928,' reads Sir Michael.

'I'm fairly sure,' says Charles, 'that the spring tide will flow under London Bridge whether we support it or not. Could we please find out who thought that was a good use of funds?' Sir Michael puts a question mark next to it.

'27th March. Private charter Aberdeen–Northolt– Aberdeen to attend Maundy Service, £30,423; 29th July 2023. King visits Healing Oxygen Hub, £18,946.'

'Bally hell,' I say, looking at Charles, '£18,000? That's quite some oxygen! How would you rate your levels of healed-ness after? Low, medium or high?' He looks confused and I remember he's never been asked to fill out a customer review question-naire. I pat him on the arm and say not to worry, it sounds perfectly lovely.

'In the year ended March 2023, the household spent £146,219 on travel to Germany for the state visit,' finishes Sir Michael, 'and a total of £1million on helicopters.'

Just then Anne pops in wearing her full Scottish tweed mufti. 'Busy morning?' I ask, grateful for a break from the privy purse.

'Fairly,' she says. 'I've visited a curling stone manu-facturer and a bottle bank in Ayr,' she continues, pour-ing herself a G&T and noticing Clive's face. 'Oh Clive, do stop looking so disapproving.' The clock strikes noon. 'It's six o'clock somewhere, so cheers! I've planted a tree at a new library, laid the foundation stone for a school and shown great, and not entirely unfeigned, interest in canal boats in Kirkintilloch. Fascinating things, canal boats,' she adds, to no one in particular. 'Very long.'

'Out of interest,' I say, 'how did you get about?'

She stares at me.

'On a horse,' she says, necking her G&T and head-ing for the door. 'Why? How do you and Charles get about? Wait, don't tell me: penny farthing?' And she leaves before Charles can tell her off. What's she doing this afternoon? I ask.

'Everything,' says Clive.

'I shudder to think,' says Charles.

2nd May
Buckingham Palace

We're on a morale-boosting visit to see the people who work in the gift shop which, as luck would have it, is right opposite the royal stables. 'Horses!' I said to Charles. 'Hurrah!' He said we're going to see people, not horses, but I put a few carrots in my handbag just in case. I asked him why morale needed boosting and he said, 'They have to make small talk about commemorative china all day, with a view of a horse's rear end.' I said, isn't that what we do? and he gave me The Look. When we get there, he does his King thing and I tell the shop assistants that some days a view of a horse's rear end would be a distinct improvement on what I'm supposed to be doing. 'Carrot, anyone?' I say offering them round, and they shuffle their feet and seem unsure what to say. We really are a terrific double act, I think to myself as we take our leave. He brings his kingly charisma and I bring carrots. Something for everyone.

'Where are we off to now?' Charles says as we get back in the car.

'Westminster City Council to hear about the super sewer,' I say, looking at my notes. 'A sewer! Imagine! Never say I don't show you a good time,' and we giggle and Clive fidgets.

'Is it the bucket seat?' I ask. 'Or us?'

5th May

Lunch with The Brig. We're in a secluded table at the back of Scott's because it makes a change from Bentleys and Bellamy's. Andrew's ordered a martini 'purely as a precaution,' he says with a twinkle, and I'm on the Chablis.

'So,' I say. 'The corker. How's it going?' and he shakes his head and leans in conspiratorially.

'I'm dating Anne Robinson,' he says and I utter a muffled shriek.

'Anne Robinson?' I say. 'The redhead? Used to do that quiz on the telly? She had a facelift, is it any good?' Andrew says that's a very random collection of things about her but yes, the redhead off the telly, and no, he has no idea if the facelift is any good or not, how does one tell such things? 'Well,' I say, 'she's about the same age as me, bit older give or take, and I look like an old bat. Does she?' and Andrew says, 'She looks lovely to me, but not as lovely as you,' and I say you old charmer, I bet you say that to all the girls and he winks at me and orders champagne.

MAY

10th May
Clarence House

Family meeting to discuss timetables for the next six months. There's me and Charles, William and Kate, Edward, who arrives for some reason on a moped with Sophie perched on the back and Anne, who arrives on horseback. She puts her mount neatly over the hedge, trots up the path and reins in outside the French windows.

'I'll sit out here,' she yells cheerfully. Charles says don't be ridiculous Anne, of course you can't attend the meeting on a horse. Anne looks put out and says why ever not, what's the matter with my horse? She pulls its ears lovingly. 'Don't you listen to what the nasty man says,' but dismounts anyway and throws the reins to the urn footman, who misses. 'Never does that with me,' I say smugly, 'but anyway, could you leave him alone? He's busy. Or at least he will be shortly.' Anne shrugs. A groom runs panting round the corner from the stables to take the horse and Anne strides through the French windows scattering mud from her boots, pulling a stray bit of straw out of her hair and making straight for the buffet. Kate smooths her immaculate skirt, crosses her legs neatly at the ankles, and looks at Anne curiously, rather as one might a rare specimen at London Zoo. Just then Clive calls the meeting to order – 'No gavel today, Clive?' I say, but he ignores me – as he quickly runs through the next week's Court Circular. I tune out until I hear

193

him say, 'The Lord de Mauley (Master of the Horse), Lieutenant Colonel Stephen Segrave (Mounted Equerries in Waiting), Captain James Boggis-Rolfe (Dismounted Equerries in Waiting) and Colonel Mark Berry (The Life Guards, Silver Stick in Waiting) were in attendance.'

'Excellent,' I say, 'well done Clive, what a good joke to lighten the atmosphere.' Everyone looks at me.

'That IS a joke,' I say. 'Isn't it? Dismounted Equerries in Waiting? Silver Stick in Waiting?' Clive says no, it is not a joke it's right here in the Court Circular. I think about reminding them how modern and slimmed down and twenty-first century we were supposed to be, then decide that now might be a good time to make a discreet trip to the window for a gasper. 'I hesitate to tell you all this,' I say, looking out, 'but Andrew's abseiling over the wall.'

'Not too late, I hope?' he bellows, striding across the lawn and Charles says no, not too late and also not invited and signals to the footman, who shoos him back through the French windows, locks them and draws the curtains.

Later

'Right,' says Clive. 'Next item on the agenda. Having not been invited to Sandringham for Christmas, Harry and Meghan are now making discreet enquiries about a possible *rapprochement* in London.'

'Discreet?' says Anne, with a most unladylike snort. 'Harry can't spell it, and Meghan doesn't understand it.'

'Well, I think a *rapprochement*'s a great idea,' says William, and everyone's jaws drop. 'Let me check my diary. How about never? Is never good for them? Are they flipping KIDDING me?' he yells, starting to turn puce and I motion to a footman to bring the dog bowl for him to kick. Charles says darling boy, at least let's hear what they have in mind and nods to Clive to continue.

'Well,' says Clive, not meeting anyone's eye, which is always a bad sign. 'They've suggested tea on the balcony at Buckingham Palace. With you all. Harry will be wearing his medals, Meghan will be wearing a nude lip and a smoky eye. And her clothes,' and here he looks down at his notes and makes quote marks in the air, 'will be luxe tailored separates by Dior Couture, link in bio. She adds that Kate can wear whatever tiara she likes because she's over tiaras. Instagram isn't interested in tiaras,' he finishes, and looks up expectantly.

'And the press coverage?' says Charles faintly. 'The royal rota? Did they have anything to say about that?'

'Yes they did, actually,' says Clive. William rolls his eyes and starts to hurl bits of dog bowl through the window, which the urn footman runs around trying to catch. 'They say that Oprah and *American Vogue* will be invited, *People* magazine will be given exclusive content and pictures and that will be sufficient, at least for them, which is all that matters. Definitely no British press. They've added that the shoot will only take half a day, they'll bring their own hair and make-up, and they own the copyright.'

The room falls silent and we all stare at each other. Anne's the first to recover.

'Marvellous,' she says, 'no problems with any of that whatsoever. Can I leave now?' And we break for the day.

11th May

We resume the timetable tedium in the afternoon after a lunch of poached salmon, which I hate, and Chablis, which I don't. I explain that perhaps there is a middle way. 'How about I invite Harry and Meghan to Ray Mill for dinner?' I say. 'Test the water as it were. No press, just me and the dogs, no hidden cameras or microphones.'

'Because they'll say "In that case what's the point",' says Charles.

'Because "Our private dinner with the Queen" will miraculously appear the following week on the cover of *People* magazine,' says William, 'with an article quoting someone "close" to the couple – look no hands!' he says, waggling his hands in the air as if to distance himself from the quotes, and giving full details of the guests, the dress code, the menu, the table decorations and where Meghan's clothes and accessories are available to buy.

'Well, I can help you right now with some of that,' I reply. 'The dress code will be Wiltshire mufti and the table decoration will be knives and forks. The guests will be me and the dogs, and the menu will be roast chicken. Can't go wrong with a roast chicken,' I say wistfully, thinking about how many blasted poached salmons at tedious functions I've had to face in my life. Sophie nods.

'Just shove it in the Aga and forget about it,' she says, and I tell her I couldn't put it better myself. She's a good gel, Sophie. Edward would never have got away with *It's a Royal Knockout* on her watch.

28th May
Highgrove, the night after the dinner
at Ray Mill with Harry and Meghan

I'm debriefing Charles about the dinner.

'The chicken was delicious if I say so myself,' I say. 'Always worth paying extra for the corn-fed from M&S. True, I dropped the bally thing on the floor when I was transferring it to the carving board, but Bluebell only gave it a bit of a going over and Beth was happy enough with a chunk out of the leg. Meghan was a bit odd, though,' I tell him. 'Harry walked in and said "Yo" and left it at that, but I didn't have a clue what Meghan was on about half the time. I think it might have had something to do with social media. She kept talking about content and "followers", but search me if I understood. Anyway, the gist of it is they're happy to come back as long as they get an apology from all of us for everything, front row on the balcony and top billing at future events.'

'What do they think this is?' says Charles. 'The Golden Globes?'

3rd June

Clive arrives bright and early with a copy of *People* magazine. 'My private dinner with the Queen by Duchess Meghan!' reads the cover, alongside a fetching photograph of Duchess Meghan herself.

'Is she sporting a smoky eye and a nude lip?' I say, smiling, and Clive says this is no laughing matter. 'Also "my" private dinner with the Queen? I'm sure they both came,' I say, 'even though all Harry said was "Yo".' Clive says Harry's presence is clearly not relevant to either *People* magazine or Meghan and it would be unseemly to speculate as to which. Then he reads out the text of the article.

'A source close to the couple, who might be called Omid Scobie, confirmed that the Queen was dressed down and the table was plainly decorated—'

'Fair dos,' I say. 'Wiltshire mufti is nothing if not dressed down and I couldn't even manage a bunch of flowers from the garden. Bally Bluebell dug up all the bulbs in the spring.'

'The two of them discussed how badly the royal family has been struggling since Meghan's departure,' continues Clive, 'and how desperately they would like to persuade them to return to the royal fold, to boost their flagging presence on social media and paltry number of followers. Duchess Meghan,' Clive continues from the magazine, 'wore an understated smoky eye and nude lip out of respect for her humble country surroundings, and luxe tailored separates by new Los Angeles-based brand HMKit, stocked by all good retailers and available to buy direct, link in bio.'

'See what I mean?' I say. 'What does that mean, link in bio? That's the sort of thing she says, out loud, looking earnest. And is HMKit really what it's called? Wouldn't have given it house room myself. She was head-to-toe in cream cashmere. The dogs would have had a field day and I'd have splashed gravy on it before I even sat down. The whole get-up reeked of dry clean only, and who's got the time for dry cleaners, instead of shove it all in a 40-degree express wash and hope for the best?'

'I thought that was what you did with roast chicken?' says Charles, 'and what's cream cashmere got to do with it? And darling one, you don't need to bother with dry cleaners. That's what these people are for,' and he gestures vaguely around the room, but there's only Clive who looks behind him, but there's no one there. 'Don't worry, Clive,' I tell him, 'I won't give you my mufti to pop down to Johnsons Cleaners.

I don't think they have many branches on The Mall anyway.'

7th June

To Birkhall for a few days' break

'Break from what?' said Annabel.

'Oh, do give it a rest,' I told her.

'Remind me,' I say to Clive on the way, 'is it a house, a castle, a palace or none of the above?'

'Officially, it's a bungalow,' says Clive, 'albeit one which has been extensively remodelled.'

'And unofficially?' I ask.

'A turreted twenty-bedroom Grade I listed castle with nine reception rooms, spread over six floors.'

'You're so clever,' I tell him as we sweep up to the front steps and the butler comes out to greet us.

'Your Majesties,' he says, 'welcome to your humble abode.' Bluebell and Beth jump out of the car behind us and give him a playful nip on each ankle. I apologise and he says, 'Not at all, ma'am, we both know that it could have been much worse,' and they trot inside in search of something to hump. I yell a precautionary 'OFF' but they ignore me and disappear.

'Nicest bungalow in Scotland,' says Charles happily, heading upstairs.

18th June

Ray Mill House

Sunday morning, and I'm in my happy place. I'm wearing my Wiltshire mufti and sitting in the dog bed next to the Aga with Bluebell and Beth and a chicken.

'About the chicken,' says Annabel, wandering in without knocking.

'It's gone rogue,' I tell her. 'Chickens do, sometimes. It's to do with the phases of the moon.' Annabel stares at me.

'Eh?' she says. 'Chickens don't have phases of the moon.'

'Fergie says they do,' I tell her and Annabel gapes. 'Don't gape, dear,' I tell her. 'Terribly vulgar.'

'Fergie?' she says. 'You've been talking to Fergie? About chickens and the moon?'

'Well,' I explain, stroking the chicken, 'she came to complain that it's freezing cold in winter at Royal Lodge, not to talk about chickens. Charles has installed smart meters so he can turn down the heating remotely. He says it's to reduce costs and save the planet but it's frightfully funny to watch. The footmen have hacked into the CCTV in the boiler room so Charles sits in his study miles away turning the thermostat down, and we watch Andrew standing there in his garter robes trying to turn it back up again and going puce. It's a scream. We could sell tickets. Anyway,' I say, warming to my theme, 'once I'd assured Fergie that it was a complete mystery why Royal Lodge is so cold, she noticed the depressed chicken on my lap and said that putting crystals in the chicken coop might help them to cope.' Annabel jabs her finger at me.

'If you take Fergie's crystals anywhere near a bally chicken coop, it'll be on the front page of the *Daily Mail* faster than you can write "Fergie: I howl at the full moon with Queen Camilla", and that is not something any of us wants Clive to read over his Earl Grey.'

'Clive?' I say. 'What about Charles?' Annabel rolls her eyes. 'You can manage Charles,' she says, 'and besides, he's probably got a few crystals about the place himself, no no—' she says, holding her hand up to stop me speaking, 'deniability. When the *Daily Mail* torture me for knowledge of your husband's crystal habits, I don't want to know anything. Clive, on the other hand, will take a very dim view of you and Fergie bonding over crystals and if you start talking about the phases of the moon he'll pack you off to Anne for re-education.'

Just then the Brig sticks his head round the door and saves the day. 'Anyone for a stiffie?' he bellows. The dogs go berserk, the chicken flees, Annabel and I shout 'Hurrah!' and Andrew salutes smartly and comes in.

22nd June

Clarence House

Meeting with the staff of my new charity, The Queen's Reading Room. I want to encourage everyone to read more, I tell them. I love books, but the young seem to spend their life on screens and it's not healthy.

'Beatrix Potter!' I tell them, 'The Brontës! Dickens! Shakespeare! Jane Austen!' They say absolutely ma'am, and how about something more modern, more diverse? 'Jilly Cooper!' I shout, almost punching the air, then remember that Charles hates it when I shout. 'I mean: Jilly Cooper,' I say in low and carefully modulated tones and the team says absolutely ma'am, they'll work on it all and get back to me.

'And about the room where we're going to film your introduction,' says the chief executive as they get up to leave and I say yes, the yellow room at Clarence House.

'It's a lovely room,' she says cautiously, 'but the researcher says that, um, there aren't any books in it?' I think about it for a moment and say yes, that's probably right. 'But there's a bally nice painting of a horse on the wall,' I tell her cheerfully, 'and a coffee-table book about the Crown Jewels. And there's always a copy of the *Racing Post* about the place if that helps?' The chief exec asks if the Crown Jewels book is the one with big pictures and no words and stuffed with pink Post-its marking the things I want to wear. Yes of course it is, I told her, what would be the point otherwise in having a book about the Crown Jewels? I don't want to read about the bally things, I want them here, on my head, I say, pointing at my head, and on my arms, I say, waving my arms like windmills, and she says of course ma'am, she quite understands. 'I'll focus group which books might inspire, and libraries where we could film it, and get back to you.' How about Duke Humfrey's Library at the Bodleian in Oxford? I ask and she says well ma'am, the light isn't great, what with it being medieval and all. 'And a medieval room in a medieval library in a medieval university is a little . . .' she tails off.

'Medieval?' I suggest.

'Exclusive,' she says, 'elitist. Whereas we're all about inclusive. I'm thinking Peckham.'

'What's Peckham?' I ask and she says it's a place in south London. It used to be gritty, she carries on, but it's now reassuringly not. It has a Gail's and a modern library which won lots of awards. 'None of them,' she adds, with an encouraging smile, 'for being medieval.'

'Goodness,' I say, heading for the window. 'Peckham! Whatever next?'

23rd June

'Peckham?' I say to Charles the following morning.

'Bless you,' he replies.

205

'No, what does Peckham mean to you?' I ask. I'm at my dressing table and he's hanging upside down.

'Hmm,' he says, thinking about it. 'Peckham. The cad in *Pride and Prejudice*?'

'That's Wickham,' I say. He grunts and Bear opens one eye to look at him, then shuffles away from under the picture rail as a precaution. 'Peckham's a place,' I say, 'used to be gritty but now reassuringly not. There's a Gail's and a library,' I tell him, 'and I filmed in it.'

'Filmed what?' says Charles. 'I didn't know you were filming anything.' I explain it's an introduction to my Reading Room charity, my attempt to get everyone reading Jilly Cooper as soon as possible.

'Good-oh,' says Charles equably. 'Don't forget that Shakespeare has his moments too, not just Jilly. And Alan Titchmarsh wrote a wonderful book about herbaceous borders, waxed quite lyrical about his delphiniums. But Peckham? Whatever next?'

'Quite so,' I reply, turning back to the mirror and letting loose an enthusiastic burst of Elnett over the wings. Charles closes his eyes, takes a deep breath in and holds it, and Bear puts his paws over his nose and squints accusingly at me through his fringe. I give the Elnett a final flourish and look at them quizzically in the mirror. 'Was it something I said?' I ask, and Bear sneezes and behind him there's a thump. 'Ow,' says Charles.

24th June
Clarence House

Charles sat me down last night with a stiff glass of Picpoul and said, 'I'm afraid I have some bad news.' My heart sank.

'Oh god,' I say, 'not the dogs?' And he says no, not the dogs. 'The children?' I say and he says no, not the children. 'Has Ray Mill burned down? Did I forget to take the chicken out of the Aga?' and he says no, it's much worse than that, it's a long-haul flight. I neck my Picpoul and put my glass out for a refill but there's no one there. The urn footman sees me through the window and tries to raise the alarm.

'Don't you move a muscle!' I yell, and Charles winces. 'Someone else can fill it. I'm going to need you any minute now.'

'We're going to Australia on a state tour for ten days next month,' says Charles very quickly, without drawing breath, anxious to get it over with. I raise an eyebrow. 'Clive and I went to the library a few months ago and had another walk round,' he says, pausing to gasp, 'and the Foreign Office very much want us to go to Australia to shore up support for the monarchy.' He gulps.

'Is there any?' I say and Charles says any what? Any Australia? I say no, support for the monarchy, but he's gasping for breath and gesturing vaguely at the drinks tray for someone to pour.

'We're going to mark the bicentenary of the New

South Wales parliament,' he says when he's taken a sip.

'Oh goody,' I mutter under my breath, 'I can barely wait.' Charles says what? And I say nothing darling, do go on.

'And we're going to commission a major piece of Aboriginal artwork,' he says. 'Or perhaps we're just going to look at a major piece of Aboriginal artwork? Which sounds more plausible?' I look blank because who the bally hell except Clive knows what we're going to do with the bally art? 'And,' says Charles with an encouraging smile, because he thinks this might actually please me, 'we're going to visit Taronga Zoo.'

'Do they have horses?' I ask suspiciously. Charles says he doesn't think so, he thinks it's more of a koala-wombat kind of place but he'll check. I look mutinous so he plays his trump card. 'There'll be a state banquet,' he says. 'You can get the rocks out.'

27th June

First major planning meeting for the state visit to the Far East

'It isn't the Far East,' says Charles, who's working through his Red Box, 'the Far East is China and Japan. We're going to Australia and New Zealand.'

'Whatever,' I say airily, waving a hand in what I assume is the opposite direction to Wiltshire. 'Do I look like the sort of gel who got geography O Level?

Can we call it the far south? Or the Horridly Hot and Far Away, Ha Ha for short?' Charles glares and says can I please stick to calling it Australia and New Zealand because otherwise the papers will hear about it and then there'll be hell to pay. The librarian is here as well, wanting some pointers about my wardrobe.

'What did Anne take with her on her last big trip?' I ask and she says a battered copy of *Black Beauty* and the Tattersalls catalogue.

'Good woman,' I say, 'but I meant clothes-wise.'

'Ah, yes,' says the librarian, consulting her notes. 'Some sunglasses which cost £2.99 at TK Maxx, a spare pair of jodhpurs and a ball of string.'

I sigh again. Anne's wardrobe isn't going to cut it.

'How about more of the trusty fit-and-flare coat dresses?' I ask hopefully and the librarian says it'll be 35 degrees in the shade and they might be a bit hot. 'What if they were cotton?' I ask and she shakes her head and says she thinks we need to go back to the drawing board on this one.

'I really couldn't agree more,' I say, losing patience. 'Let's go back to the drawing board where this bally trip was first mapped out, stamp on it, chop it into bits and chuck it on the fire,' and Charles groans and Clive walks in and says is there anything wrong?

'Nothing at all,' I say. 'The Foreign Office have changed their mind, they want us to go to Wiltshire now, not the Far East, and stay there quietly until after Christmas. In Wiltshire mufti,' I add for good measure.

'Nice try,' says Clive, closing the door.

28th June

Harry's flown over out of the blue to talk.

'About himself?' I ask Clive. 'Or other people?' He suppresses a smile and mutters something non-committal. 'He's requested a one-on-one with His Majesty,' says Clive, 'without me. Or you.' There's a pause and I look at Clive and he looks at me and I motion to the urn footman to take up position. 'Oh no, I think wicked stepmothers should definitely be in attendance,' I say, quoting Harry's book, *Spare*, 'if only to see him squirm. And you need to be there so I don't have to throw him out when he starts whingeing about whatever he's upset about at the moment. All in all, it's looking less like a one-on-one and more like tea for four in the morning room when he arrives, don't you think? Or would you prefer coffee, Clive?'

The meeting went as well as can be expected. Harry said he was here to serve, and Clive said, 'Whom?' Then Harry said he'd be willing to do the occasional royal job and Clive said which royal jobs did you have in mind? There's an investiture at Windsor a week on Tuesday, shouldn't be any more than seven hours on your feet making polite small talk with a succession of strangers. Or how about the new council offices in Darlington? Anne's due to open those next month, but I'm sure she'd be happy to delegate. Harry said he was thinking more Trooping the Colour, Remembrance Sunday, fly-past on the balcony and wave to the cheering crowds, that sort of thing.

Charles said he'd think about it, Clive said time to go and I ambled over to the window for a ciggie.

29th June

'You have an 11 a.m. meeting with the Crown Jeweller and an actual stylist, not a librarian, to discuss gems and looks for the Australia tour,' says Clive and I say oh Clive, let's call a spade a spade: not gems, rocks, man, rocks! Gems sounds like it might be contagious, 'And besides,' I add, 'humour me, rocks are my only reason to be cheerful in the face of a twenty-four-hour flight of unimaginable constant terror which may end at any time with our plummeting from the skies to a fiery death.' Clive says that's exceptionally unlikely and starts to explain the laws of physics and how planes stay in the air and I hold up my hand to stop him. 'I do not care,' I tell him. 'Do I look like the sort of gel who understands physics? The point is, who would care for Bluebell and Beth if I weren't here?' Clive starts unconvincingly to say any number of people and I shut him down with a glare. 'The answer is nobody would take care of them, or at least not as well as me, and no one will ever convince me that going somewhere that is completely inaccessible by horse is ever a good idea.' Clive, who knows when to concede defeat, bows and leaves me to the Crown Jeweller.

'Your Majesty!' says the Crown Jeweller and I tell him yes, come in, so which rocks are we thinking? The aquamarines? He says he's taken advice from the Foreign Office. My face falls. Advice from the FO is never what you want to hear. 'I don't have a choice, ma'am,' he says sympathetically, 'we have to honour our guests, not cause a diplomatic incident and the fact is that Australia is most famous for its opals.' I look at him aghast. 'Opals?' I say, 'But opals are dismal. Nobody wants to wear opals. They don't come in carats. They're not aquamarines or diamonds or sapphires. Please, please tell me we haven't got any opals in the collection, so I have to wear the aquamarines instead?' The man looks crestfallen and says well actually we do have some opals, but they don't get worn much.

'Go figure,' I tell him and he looks startled at my turn of phrase. 'Learnt it from Meghan,' I say despondently. 'Useful phrase when people talk about opals and I have to aim for stoic.'

The jewel man leaves and the styling team arrives to discuss outfits for the tour, *sans* librarian, which seems a bit pointed of Clive. I make a mental note later to tell him he really should read more. Anyway there's darling Fiona for day wear, darling Philip for the hats, darling Bruce for evening and bally Annabel for straight talking.

'What are you doing here?' I say. 'It's frocks today,

not modular sofas, and the velvet pouffe situation is under control.' She says Clive invited her. Anyway, I tell them, I've been thinking about my look a lot, which surprises them.

'I've reached a decision,' I say. 'They're very casual in Australia,' I say to a line of expectant faces, and one face with pursed lips, 'so I'm thinking Wiltshire mufti, but linen, and Philip can put corks round the brim of the hats. Practical, and an elegant homage to our host country, no? The Foreign Office will love it.'

Annabel un-purses her lips. 'Ha ha,' she says, 'very funny.' Philip sags with relief that I was joking, even though I wasn't, not entirely.

'Just my little joke,' I say to lighten the atmosphere. 'So, fit-and-flare for day, plenty of zips up the front, and Bruce,' I say turning to him, 'your usual magic, if you please.'

'Delighted, ma'am,' he says, bowing. 'And no animals embroidered on these dresses.'

I note he puts it as a statement, not a question and seize my chance. Actually Charlotte's got a new pony, I tell him, so how about that? Bruce looks helplessly at Annabel, who gives me a warning look. 'Joke,' I say, even though it wasn't.

'How about a couple of koalas?' Annabel gives me a hard stare.

'A wombat? Anyone? No?'

30th June

House party at Sandringham

Charles has gone fishing to break the monotony of talking about the Far East.

Everyone thinks we spend every weekend hunting, shooting and fishing, I once said to Fiona, but it's a little-known fact that I can't really be doing with shooting. It frightens the horses. Fishing's too wet, and nobody in their right mind wants to eat trout, and hunting's tremendous fun but they won't let me do it any more in case I fall off. 'But I'm excellent at the *après* shoot,' I reassured Charles. 'I think it plays to my strengths.'

'Which are?' he says.

'I'll get back to you with a full list,' I tell him with a twinkle, 'but it definitely includes a hearty lunch and six o'clock stiffies.'

William and Kate have popped over from Anmer to check on the arrangements. 'I thought Anne was coming?' says William, running a pen down the guest list.

'I hope that pen isn't one of your father's,' I tell him. 'And yes, she was coming. But then she got invited to a reception for Royal Warrant Holders at Reading town hall and a dinner on a boat up the Thames to celebrate the forty-fifth anniversary of something or other. When I asked her what they were celebrating she looked vague and said, 'Boats? The Thames? Does it matter?' and I said no, probably not, and just then a groom walked round the corner and I said oh look, a horse! Anne looked at me oddly and said 'I know'.

'She is a marvel,' says William. 'A Saturday night reception at Reading town hall! What would we do without her?'

'Run away,' says Kate.

'Struggle,' I tell him.

'Remind me what it was that Andrew said in that *Newsnight* interview about the paedophile he invited for a shooting weekend?' I ask William and he groans. 'He looked affronted at any suggestion of impropriety and said it was just a perfectly straightforward shooting weekend,' and I chuckle and say ah yes, Andrew, man of the people, 'Although,' I muse, 'given what that Epstein chap was up to I suppose we should be relieved that he didn't describe it as a deviant shooting weekend with optional S&M after dinner.' William looks at me appalled and says please don't say things like that out loud, in public, ever. Someone might hear.

I shrug and log on to my Betfair account on the iPad. 'Boom!' I say, punching the air. 'I won fifty quid on the two-forty-five at Sandown!' William looks at me appalled for the second time in ten seconds, and starts to say please don't ... but I give him my most quelling look, close the iPad and head to the window for a celebratory fag.

'The Crown Jeweller is back, Your Majesty,' says the footman, 'to discuss options for the visit to Australia and New Zealand.' 'Marvellous,' I say, 'show him in. Lovely man,' I add to Annabel, 'still no idea what his name is, but he's ever so good with his hands. Carved up our crowns quite brilliantly so they sit on our big old bonces. Just don't mention the Koh-i-Noor. Makes him sweat.' The Crown Jeweller walks in looking apprehensive, and Annabel reaches for the coffee-table book. Another footman takes up position behind me with a fresh pack of bright pink Post-it notes on a silver salver.

'Righto, page 104,' I say to kick things off and the Crown Jeweller, whatever his name is, looks confused. 'Page 104?' he says. 'Of what?'

'The Crown Jewels book, man!' says Annabel impatiently, waving her copy at him, which is quite something given how heavy it is. 'Haven't you done your

217

homework?' and the man looks helplessly at the foot-man behind me, who I know will be looking at the ceiling, because they always do.

'Page 104,' I repeat, slowly and clearly. 'The emer-alds. All of them.'

'I haven't checked on the status of the emeralds,' he says, 'but I have excellent news about the opals.'

'Oh?' I say.

'Yes,' he says. 'They're problematic.'

Annabel rolls her eyes. 'Don't tell me, we nicked them from Australia?' and the man looks horrified.

'Of course not!' he says. 'Or at least, not exactly. But the Australian opal mines in the nineteenth century were not, er, manned by, er, highly paid individuals who chose to be there, precisely, or in the fruit of whose labours we can now freely rejoice.'

Annabel looks at me. 'Do you have any idea what he's on about?' and I shrug.

'Spit it out,' she says to him.

'Convicts,' he says. 'Could I perhaps offer you ladies a suite of rubies instead? Or turquoise? We have some lovely and very unproblematic turquoise in the collec-tion. Pearls, too. And,' he checks his phone, which pings, 'Ah yes, marvellous. The emeralds are now available. They've been held in a secret and secure location for many years because Prince Harry once indicated that Meghan would be happy to accept them as a gift.' He starts to describe the turquoise and pearls and Annabel looks at him as if he's mad and says, 'Yes, but what PAGE are they on, man, what PAGE? We need pictures, not words!'

And then the man surprises us both. He looks at Annabel, rallies himself, stands up straight and says, 'Madam. I have no idea what page they're on. I do not have a copy of your coffee-table book about the Crown Jewels, because I do not need one. I am the Crown Jeweller, not a sales assistant at Waterstones. But what I can tell you is that the items you're talking about are in stand number 204, room 47, level 2, up the stairs and behind the door on the right, next to some exquisite sapphires of unusually impeccable provenance, in His Majesty's Royal Palace and Fortress of The Tower of London, Tower Hill, London EC3.'

There's a stunned silence during which Annabel peers at him over her half-moon glasses with new admiration. Then she turns and looks at me with raised eyebrows.

'Bally well done,' I say, giving the jeweller the double thumbs up. 'See you there next Tuesday. And bring the aquamarines, just in case.'

3rd August

Off to Scotland soon, so off to Bellamy's for a cosy lunch *à deux* with The Brig. I suggested Mosimann's when we arranged it over the phone, or Bentleys, but he said how about Bellamy's for a change? 'They're so discreet you could have rampant rumpy-pumpy in the middle of the dining room and it wouldn't get into the papers,' he said. I had to speak sharply to him and say that talking on the phone to your ex-wife about rampant rumpy-pumpy wasn't really the done thing. He said oh lighten up, you know what I mean and I said, 'Yes, I do, you mean rampant rumpy-pumpy so just stop it, who knows who's listening in. And calling me Lorraine isn't funny any more now I actually am La Reine and if it gets out Charles will be furious,' but he just laughed. 'Feeling feisty today, are we?' he says and I tell him to shut up and put the phone down.

'I'll have the artichoke and green bean salad with no dressing, then steamed Dover sole, no Hollandaise,' I tell the waiter when he comes to take our order. Andrew orders egg and bacon croquettes and steak frites with Béarnaise, extra frites and creamed spinach on the side. 'You're obviously not worried about your waistline,' I say ruefully, telling him about the new wardrobe I've got to fit into for the Far East or the Near East or the Deep South or whichever hot hell-hole it is we're going to.

'I'll be working it all off,' he says with a wink. 'I've met a new lady friend, Serena, aka the beauty from Djibouti.'

'Is she really from Djibouti?' I ask, thinking of the corker from Majorca who was no such thing. He says no of course not, she's from Sheffield. He orders a half-bottle of Chablis for me and a bottle of Pauillac for himself and proceeds to regale me with tales of life in Gloucestershire, which seem to consist mostly of gardening and rumpy-pumpy and occasionally both together.

'I won't see you for weeks now,' I tell him later, as we say our goodbyes. 'We're off to Scotland for a few weeks, then I've got to go to the Deep South and look delighted.'

'Really?' he says. 'I thought you were going to Australia and New Zealand?'

'That's the one,' I say, waving in the direction of Green Park. 'Will the beauty from Djibouti still be in the picture when I'm back?'

'Shouldn't think so,' says Andrew cheerfully. 'I've already got the hottie from Haiti waiting in the wings.'

'And where's she from?' I ask, as my protection officer opens the car door for me.

'Basingstoke,' he says, giving my bottom an affectionate squeeze and striding away up Bruton Place. 'Behave yourself in Australia!' he shouts over his shoulder. 'Chin up and don't forget to look delighted!' I roll my eyes and get in the car.

4th September
Birkhall

Quiet Monday night in with Charles and the dogs before we head back to London and the horrors of the Deep South next month. Annabel's here too, because she came with us on our honeymoon and never really left.

'Do you know,' I tell her, 'Birkhall is the only turreted bungalow in Scotland?' and she says what on earth are you talking about? I fill her in on Clive's clever reclassification exercise.

'But that's genius,' she says, 'we could reclassify all sorts of things.'

'Like what?' I ask her.

'You,' she says. 'We could reclassify you as a teetotal non-smoker. It has a certain ring to it, no?' Tonight Charles and I are doing *The Times* crossword. He insists on doing it in print but I do it on the iPad so I can cheat. While he chooses a pen, I scan Clive's dossier on what I'm going to be doing

223

over the next week or so: planting a tree in Kent, visiting a hospital in Surrey, opening a new refuge for victims of domestic violence and touring the newsroom of the *Sun*.

'Do you realise I'm supposed to be touring the newsroom of the *Sun* next week?' I say to Charles and he looks up, alarmed.

'Why?' he says. 'What have you done?'

I cast my mind back to Andrew patting my bottom outside Bellamy's in the summer, and talking about rumpy-pumpy on the phone, then reflect that everything is usually alright in the end, except when it isn't.

'Nothing,' I say. 'I expect they just want me to look delighted.'

'Nobody does it better,' says Charles, gazing at me affectionately. 'Not even me.'

'Especially not you when you're trying to find a pen,' I tell him, and jot down a note to dig out my new journal when we get back to London. The first one Annabel bought me is nearly full. The new one is bottle green with 'Golf Notes' stamped on the front.

'But I don't play golf,' I told Annabel when she gave it to me.

'I know,' she said, 'but it's green, so it matches the soft furnishings. The alternative was orange, which does not. It also had THE BOSS stamped on it, which you are not.'

'Oh how thoughtful, did you get that one for Charles?' I asked and she looked at me in astonishment.

'Don't be ridiculous,' she said. 'I got it for Clive.' This evening, sitting comfortably at Birkhall, in a refreshingly Clive-free space, I reflect that she was probably right. I look fondly over at Charles, who's chosen a pen, and give the thumbs up to Annabel.

'Right,' I say to them, 'are we ready? Where were we? Five across . . .'

Acknowledgements

This book grew out of a feature I wrote for *The Times*. My editor wanted something fun about Camilla's first year as Queen and we hit on a spoof diary. I cast the Queen in a Bridget Jones mould, armed her with stiff drinks, cigarettes and cans of Elnett, and it pretty much wrote itself. Thank you, then, to Helen Fielding for her work of rare genius and to Nicola Jeal, an editor of rare genius.

That was a year ago. I always assumed that writing a book was beyond me but my agent, Eugenie Furniss, made it seem like a possibility, and Andreas Campomar at Little, Brown has made it a reality. Thank you so much to them both, and to my friends Paul, Rupert and Clare, who drove me round the bend saying 'do it' until I did.

I owe a huge debt to Beatrix Potter. My father used to read me her Peter Rabbit books before I could read them myself, and they were the first I ever loved. Her paintings and drawings get all the attention and they are, obviously, magical. But it was her equally magical prose which captivated me when I was little and still does now I'm not.

Finally, I apologise to the Queen for being cheeky and to nearly everyone else in the book, especially Annabel and Clive, for inventing characters which I'm sure are many miles from the truth. Prince Andrew, I'm afraid you have no one to blame but yourself.